CW01508642

BRANDING TERROR

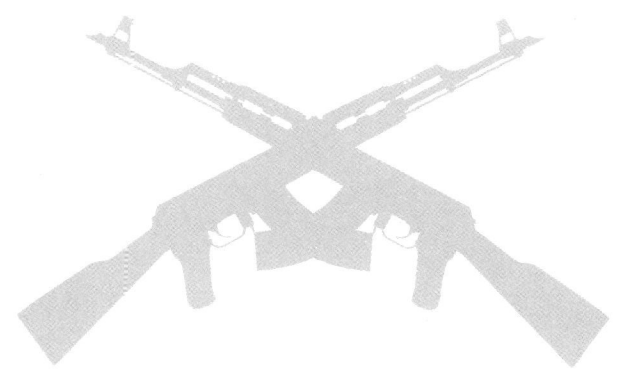

BRANDING TERROR

Artur Beifuss • Francesco Trivini Bellini

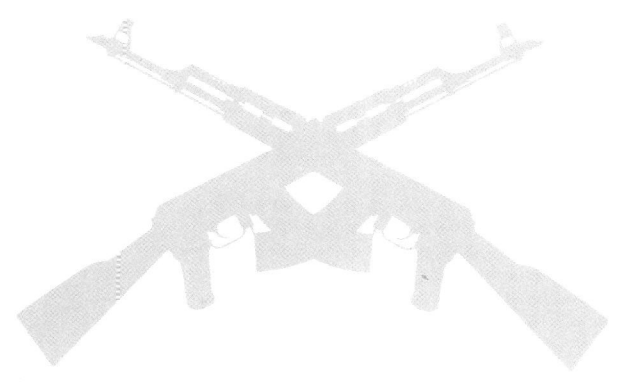

The Logotypes and Iconography of Insurgent Groups and Terrorist Organizations

Foreword by Steven Heller

LONDON • NEW YORK

FOREWORD

Steven Heller

Any irregular fighting force can technically be seen as a terrorist organization. Historically, uniformed combatants have followed set rules of engagement, while terrorists, who usually do not wear uniforms, make their own rules on how to surprise, disrupt and terrorize non-combatants. Regular army or police units are often at a disadvantage when battling un-uniformed guerrilla fighters: who is the enemy and who the innocent bystander? A recognizable uniform implies that the wearer follows battlefield conventions; this, among other things, suggests that he or she does not target civilians. Without military markings, anarchy prevails.

Terrorists (or freedom fighters, depending on one's perspective) may, in the manner of Los Angeles street gangs, in fact display identifying marks, signs or symbols, such as special tattoos or clothes. But members are careful not to reveal them overtly, lest they betray their mission and their comrades.

Those whom we call terrorists, even the most ragtag rebels, wherever they reside, usually have a cause they are fighting for. Some groups carry out violent acts; others engage in the cultural, social or political process while also allying themselves with violent groups or committing violent acts themselves. In those nations where free speech is non-existent, secrecy is not just a virtue, it is also necessary for survival. Yet this does not preclude the existence of some sort of identifying mark. Every military or political organization – outlawed or not – in the world has maintained a 'brand identity' over time. This book is about those groups whose brand identities, histories and legends have purposefully been made public. In countries around the globe, there are scores of groups and organizations branded as terrorist that use graphic-design idioms to express their respective crusades. Some designs are more elaborate than others, relating more to medieval coats of arms than to modern trademarks, while others are striking in their economy. Some of the organizations may be familiar from news reports, others (sometimes splinter groups) are unknown to most people. What they all seem to have in common is a defining logo that emerges when needed, to distinguish one group from another.

A logo is the essential point of contact between the public and any product, organization or movement. What would the Catholic church be without the crucifix (which began as an outlawed symbol)? Could Adolf Hitler have commanded the German nation without ritualizing the swastika (which is outlawed in Germany today)? And where would the United States be without the Stars and Stripes, and all the complementary American national iconography? Of course, business logos are considered to be 'sacred': the Coca-Cola, IBM and Apple marks, for example, are protected at all costs from infringement by corporate terrorists and industrial saboteurs.

A successful logo is imbued with unequal parts of mythology and truth, as well as all the other positive virtues that a product or idea needs in order to thrive. Logos may lose their potency, but even the most impotent have meaning for someone. They are charged badges of loyalty. But even more, a logo is the glue that binds disparate individuals into a unified mass. Regardless of the quality of design, an effective logo is both a bonding agent for those of similar leaning and a key to the realm that excludes the non-believers or the otherwise unwelcome. Just look at how many T-shirts and other apparel are marketed for their logos.

This book contains a curious amalgam of the mundane and the extraordinary. Some of the branding devices are clichéd, displaying too many eagles and guns, in the same way that ovals and stars are overused in American corporate branding; others trigger fear, especially when seen close up. Some seem benign, as in the case of Aum Shinrikyo's peace dove (p. 83); others embrace violence, as with the crossed swords of the Muslim Brotherhood (p. 235). Taken out of context, some are simply enigmatic: Ansar al-Islam's flags (p. 71) neither frighten nor inflame. The aesthetic qualities, too, vary. The simple beauty of the Army of Muhammad flag (p. 79) belies the nature of a group that has attacked Indian interests in Kashmir, killing several hundred people. Compare that to Jemmah Anshorut Tauhid's kitsch seal (p. 187), which has all the graphic noise of a shareware cut-rate-logo internet site. Alas, certain groups have become too reliant on tricks of the computer. The flag and logos for the Liberation Tigers of Tamil Eelam, for example (pp. 215 and 217), suffer from too many Photoshop filters and options. Then there is the flag of green featuring a yellow star inside a red circle, as professionally impressive as any in this book, devised by the deadly National Democratic Front of Bodoland (currently in negotiations with the Indian government to resolve differences; p. 239).

The extreme violence committed in the name of these logos makes writing about them in terms of aesthetics or production values seem silly and irrelevant. Yet these terrorist groups are all brands, and are given a certain viability through branding methods. Branding is a tool that has no conscience or morality – it can be used for good or bad, and sometimes for both in tandem. These images exist to trigger a moral response. What may seem unthreatening could be a symbolic means to reduce the horror (even to appear to be official, or produced by a government-in-waiting). And what appears to be quite threatening may be a symbolic way to strike fear in the enemy and reinforce allegiance in the follower.

INTRODUCTION

Artur Beifuss

In October 2006 the Reuters news agency released a photograph showing an Israeli explosives expert holding the remains of an explosives-laden Al-Quds 3 rocket, which had been fired from the Gaza Strip (part of the Palestinian territories) and had landed near the Israeli town of Sderot. Interestingly, the accompanying report centred not on the rocket launch itself or the casualties, but on the 'branding' associated with the missile. Reuters reported that, in an effort to receive the 'credit' for the attack, the group responsible, Islamic Jihad Movement in Palestine (IJMP; p. 171), had inscribed the rocket in Hebrew to make sure that it would be 'distinguished from those of other groups', such as Hamas (p. 129) or the al-Aqsa Martyrs Brigades (p. 37).

This episode illustrates the extent to which the field of terrorism is contested. With numerous active groups around the world (several of them having a similar ideology and the same goals), 'branding' and 'marketing' become important elements of the terrorist group's overall strategy. Getting credited for an attack is almost as important as the attack itself. The rocket attack against Sderot by IJMP was a terrorist act, but it was also an act of visual communication designed to brand the identity of the group, communicate what it stands for and what its capabilities are, and create an 'experience' between individuals and the organization.

Branding, marketing and the visual communication of ideas and messages are tools that are used not only by corporations and political parties. Every organization that tries to put a message across, to influence an audience and to stand out in a highly competitive sector, or even to mark a claimed territory – as in the contested regions of Palestine and Northern Ireland – needs a well-defined visual identity. The use of symbols, colour and typography codes a well-designed logo of a terrorist group; brands the organization; signals the ideas that lie behind the group's creation and its aims; and communicates a certain spirit in a way that speaks to the audience. The message conveyed is often one of war or resistance.

In another news story, published in the *Washington Times* in January 2008, it was reported that, in Italy, the Carioca amateur-league football club had adopted for its players' shirts the green assault-rifle logo of the Lebanese terrorist group Hezbollah (p. 145); the team had also changed its name to 'Zassbollah', a combination of 'Hezbollah' and the family name of the team's captain, Luigi Zasso. This report is a perfect example of how a logo can be adopted and used to convey a certain message. According to one Zassbollah player, the team had appropriated the Hezbollah logo in order to frighten its adversaries and to make them understand the extent to which it was prepared to fight to win a match.

The branding employed by terrorist groups is an understudied subject. Current studies of terrorism are limited to discussions on the definition of the word, and the nature and scope of terrorist acts. These studies are predominantly carried out in a subjective manner, defining terrorism as a criminal act. While this approach offers a functional means of understanding the major common elements of terrorism and helps to counter it, it does not help us to understand the brand identities of terrorist organizations, nor how their visual communication works, why certain visual elements are preferred over others, and how and why they carry certain meanings, emotions and values.

When defining what terrorism is, analysts, researchers and others working in the field of counterterrorism agree on the following: terrorism is a threat or an act of violence; the threat or act of violence is used primarily to create an atmosphere of fear and coercion; and it is a purposeful action, a form of communication designed to send an intimidating message of strength, and committed with a view to serving a political or social purpose. It follows that the aim of terrorism is to change people's behaviour. Terrorist acts are committed in order to affect public opinion, which will put pressure on decision-makers to surrender to the terrorists' demands. In essence, therefore, terrorism is a form of psychological warfare, in which the direct victim is not the primary target. However, through the threat or act of violence, not only does the terrorist organization communicate with, inform and direct the constituency from which it wants surrender, but also it informs and directs people it perceives as partners and potential recruits. When it comes to conveying its identity and message, visual communication is essential.

As was illustrated by the report on the Al-Quds 3 rocket attack on Sderot, the offensive itself, or the product the organization has to offer, is only one aspect of a terrorist group's identity. A group's name, motto, dress codes and logo are also very important visual manifestations of its identity. All these aspects are critical to the success of the organization, with success measured by the level and scope of influence on the audience. It is therefore strategically important for a terrorist organization to dedicate resources to narrowing the gap between its identity and its image, as seen from the viewpoint of its audience. In corporate communications, this is called branding. Branding a terrorist attack or a terrorist organization is a purposeful action, undertaken to attach emotional associations to an otherwise undifferentiated 'product', and to allow the audience to identify the organization and what it stands for.

It is against this backdrop that Francesco Trivini Bellini, the creative director of this book, approached me with the idea of creating a brand-identity manual of worldwide terrorist organizations. In an effort to understand better the nature of the terrorist threat itself, this book examines the visual language of terrorist organizations as conveyed through logos and other aspects of their visual communication; it is a starting point in understanding aspects of the visual identity of terrorist groups.

So as to avoid engaging in a debate about precisely which groups can or should be classified as terrorist organizations, we have used lists of designated terrorist groups established by the United States, the European Union, Australia, Russia and India. These lists are created and maintained by the respective bodies tasked with national security and counterterrorism. Terrorism is defined by the legislation of the respective governments. To be included on a government's official list, an organization must be deemed to pose a threat to the security of its citizens and to engage in terrorist activities, which include planning and preparation. The authorities of the United States and Australia list only foreign organizations.

Not all the groups listed by these bodies have a logo or flag. Since visual identity is the focus of this book, only those groups that have a logo or a distinctive flag are discussed in these pages. Most of the imagery shown in this book was found in 'open' sources, such as a group's website or a video it has produced; the logos and flags were then verified by at least one trustworthy source. Most of the images were not of good enough quality to be printed, and so, in order to be featured in this book they have been retraced.

For each group, we give a brief overview of its ideology, its geographical location and key dates in its history, followed by an analysis of the imagery it uses. We analyse the elements of the imagery in relation to the group's history, aims and actions; define the colour codes and graphic patterns; and translate the typography. In the course of our work to verify and validate the origins and meaning of the logotypes, as well as to describe the history of the various organizations, we have used mainly open sources – news reports, websites and books – rather than such classified sources as intelligence reports. In order to provide an objective analysis, we have attempted to use as many primary sources as possible, especially interviews with members of terrorist organizations. However, owing to the nature of terrorism and to the fact that, in many countries, disclosure of membership of a designated terrorist group is certain to lead to imprisonment, it was not always possible to access such interviews. Thus, so as to gain a deeper understanding of these groups and their visual identities, we turned to more accessible sources, including original video recordings of terrorist groups, published written communiqués, and official magazines and websites created by terrorist organizations. However, authentication of these sources is not always possible, and knowledge of the original language, as well as deductive reasoning, is required. When these types of sources were unavailable, we used secondary sources to collect information. Examples of secondary sources include peer-reviewed academic articles and books, reports by governmental and non-governmental organizations, newspaper and television reports, and information gathered from internet forums and blogs. It was not always possible to find and verify useful information, and we are aware that some inexactness may occur.

As a last point, it should be said that our effort to offer a foundation for understanding the visual identities of terrorist organizations requires that one attempts to study terrorism without immediately condemning it. This is not to be viewed as displaying insensitivity to the victims of terrorist acts, nor as an acceptance of the harmful, destructive and blameworthy motives of terrorists and their deeds.

ABOUT
THIS BOOK

Each of the groups featured in these pages has its own entry; the groups are listed in alphabetical order, and are numbered (see list on pp. 17–21). As shown below, in each entry the first page gives a general overview of the group, including when and where it was founded, its ideology and its capabilities. Subsequent pages analyse the group's logo(s) and, where relevant, its flag(s) and other imagery: right-hand pages feature a full-colour image and the analysis, left-hand pages a black-and-white outline of the image showing its individual components, as well as a colour chart identifying the colour values used in the image. However, the colours of any photographic elements in the image are omitted from the chart, as it would be impractical to list the many tones contained within such elements. In the text, the symbol » in front of a group's name indicates that it has its own entry.

First page of each entry

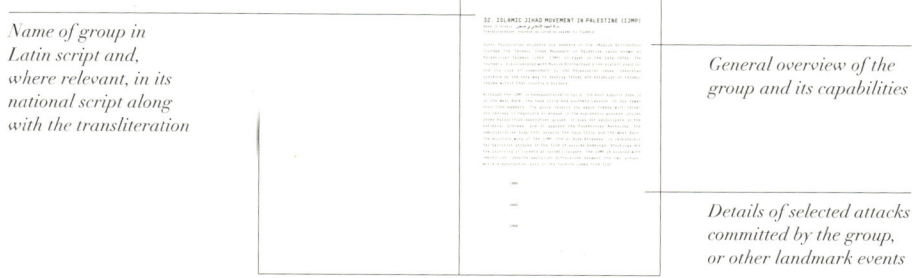

Name of group in Latin script and, where relevant, in its national script along with the transliteration

General overview of the group and its capabilities

Details of selected attacks committed by the group, or other landmark events

Subsequent pages

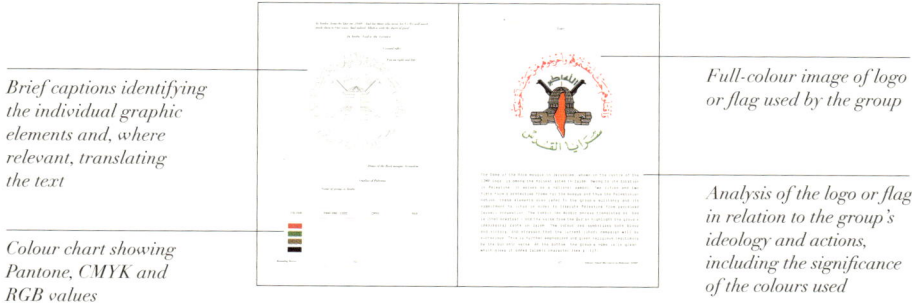

Brief captions identifying the individual graphic elements and, where relevant, translating the text

Colour chart showing Pantone, CMYK and RGB values

Full-colour image of logo or flag used by the group

Analysis of the logo or flag in relation to the group's ideology and actions, including the significance of the colours used

DESIGNATED ORGANIZATIONS

This list of designated terrorist organizations combines the official lists of Australia, the European Union, India, Russia and the United States (see p. 13). Only those organizations that have a logo or a flag are discussed in this book; these featured organizations are shown in black type on the list, and are numbered. The number given to each featured organization is used in the maps on pp. 22–27 (see guide below), to show at a glance the country in which the organization is based, and also appears on the first page of the organization's entry (pp. 29–317). Groups that are not discussed in this book are shown on this list in grey type, and are not numbered.

■ *Organizations featured in this book*

▨ *Organizations not featured in this book*

Guide to maps pp. 22–27

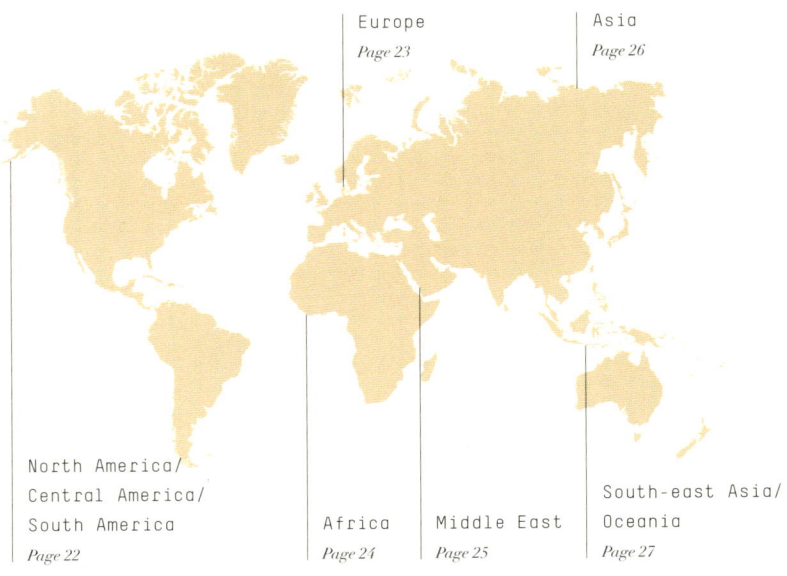

Europe
Page 23

Asia
Page 26

North America/
Central America/
South America
Page 22

Africa
Page 24

Middle East
Page 25

South-east Asia/
Oceania
Page 27

	AUSTRALIA	EU	INDIA	RUSSIA	US
/ Abu Nidal Organization		X			X
1. Abu Sayyaf Group (ASG)	X				X
/ Akhil Bharat Nepali Ekta Samaj			X		
2. Al-Aqsa Foundation (AAF)		X			
3. Al-Aqsa Martyrs Brigades (AAMB)		X			X
4. Al-Badr (AB)			X		
5. Al-Haramain Islamic Foundation (HIF)				X	
6. Al-Qaeda (AQ)	X		X	X	X
7. Al-Qaeda in Iraq (AQI)	X				X
/ Al-Qaeda in the Arabian Peninsula	X				X
8. Al-Qaeda in the Islamic Maghreb (AQIM)	X			X	X
/ Al Tafkir and al-Hijra		X			
/ Al Umar-Mujahideen			X		
/ All Tripura Tiger Force			X		
9. Ansar al-Islam (AAI)	X				X
10. Army of Islam (AOI)					X
11. Army of Muhammad (JEM)	X		X		X
/ Asbat al-Ansar				X	X
12. Aum Shinrikyo (AUM)		X			X
13. Babbar Khalsa (BKI)		X	X		
14. Basque Fatherland and Liberty (ETA)		X			X
/ Brigata XX Luglio		X			
15. Brigate Rosse per la Costruzione del Partito Comunista Combattente (BR-PCC)		X			
16. Caucasus Emirate (CE)				X	
/ Cellula Contro Capitale, Carcere i suoi Carcerieri e le sue Celle		X			
17. Communist Party of India (Maoist) (CPI-M)			X		
/ Communist Party of India People's War			X		
18. Communist Party of the Philippines (CPP) / New People's Army (NPA)		X			X

		AUSTRALIA	EU	INDIA	RUSSIA	US
/	Continuity Irish Republican Army		X			X
/	Cooperativa Artigiana Fuoco ed Affini – Occasionalmente Spettacolare		X			
/	Deendar Anjuman			X		
/	Dukhtaran-e-Millat			X		
/	Egyptian Islamic Jihad				X	
19.	Federazione Anarchica Informale (FAI)		X			
20.	Gama'a al-Islamiyya (IG)		X		X	X
21.	Great Eastern Islamic Raiders Front (IBDA-C)		X			
22.	Grupos de Resistencia Antifascista Primero de Octubre (GRAPO)		X			
23.	Hamas		X			X
24.	Harakat al-Shabaab al-Mujahideen (al-Shabaab)	X				X
/	Harakat ul-Jihad-i-Islami			X		X
/	Harakat ul-Jihad-i-Islami/Bangladesh			X		X
25.	Harakat ul-Mujahideen (HUM)	X		X		X
26.	Hezbollah					X
27.	Hizb-ut-Tahrir (HUT)				X	
28.	Hizbul Mujahideen (HM)		X	X		
29.	Hofstadgroep (HG)		X			
30.	Holy Land Foundation for Relief and Development (HLF)		X			
31.	Indian Mujahideen (IM)			X		X
/	International Sikh Youth Federation		X	X		
32.	Islamic Jihad Movement in Palestine (IJMP) (Russian list) / Palestinian Islamic Jihad (Australian, EU and US lists)	X	X		X	X
/	Islamic Jihad Union					X
33.	Islamic Movement of Uzbekistan (IMU)	X			X	X

		AUSTRALIA	EU	INDIA	RUSSIA	US
34.	Izz ad-Din al-Qassam Brigades (IDQ)	X	X			
/	Jamiat-ul-Mujahideen			X	X	
/	Jammu and Kashmir Islamic Front			X		
/	Jemaah Islam_ya Organization (Pakistan)	X				X
35.	Jemmah Anshorut Tauhid (JAT)					X
/	Jund al-Sham				X	
36.	Jundallah					X
37.	Kahane Chai / Kach		X			X
/	Kanglei Yaol Kanba Lup			X		
/	Kangleipak Communist Party			X		
38.	Kata'ib Hezbollah (KH)					X
/	Khalistan Commando Force			X		
/	Khalistan Zindabad Force		X	X		
39.	Kurdistan Freedom Falcons (TAK)		X			
40.	Kurdistan Workers' Party (PKK)	X	X			X
/	Lashkar-e-Jhangvi	X				X
41.	Lashkar-e-Toyyiba (LET)	X		X	X	X
42.	Liberation Tigers of Tamil Eelam (LTTE)		X	X		X
43.	Libyan Islamic Fighting Group (LIFG)					X
44.	Loyalist Volunteer Force (LVF)		X			
/	Manipur People's Liberation Front			X		
/	Maoist Communist Centre			X		
/	Moroccan Islamic Combatant Group					X
45.	Mujahideen-e-Khalq Organization (MEK)					X
46.	Muslim Brotherhood (MB)				X	
47.	National Democratic Front of Bodoland (NDFB)			X		
48.	National Liberation Army (ELN)		X			X
49.	National Liberation Front of Tripura (NLFT)			X		

		AUSTRALIA	EU	INDIA	RUSSIA	US
/	Nuclei Armati per il Comunismo		X			
50.	Orange Volunteers (OV)		X			
51.	Palestine Liberation Front (PLF)		X			X
/	People's Congress of Ichkeria and Dagestan				X	
52.	People's Liberation Army (PLA)			X		
/	People's Revolutionary Party of Kangleipak			X		
53.	Popular Front for the Liberation of Palestine (PFLP)		X			X
54.	Popular Front for the Liberation of Palestine — General Command (PFLP-GC)		X			X
55.	Real Irish Republican Army (Real IRA)		X			X
/	Red Hand Defenders		X			
56.	Revolutionary Armed Forces of Colombia (FARC)		X			X
57.	Revolutionary Organization 17 November (17N)		X			X
58.	Revolutionary People's Liberation Party/Front (DHKP/C)		X			X
59.	Revolutionary Struggle (EA)		X			X
60.	Shining Path (SL)		X			X
/	Social Reform Society (Kuwait)				X	
/	Society of the Revival of the Islamic Heritage				X	
/	Solidarietà Internazionale		X			
/	Students Islamic Movement of India			X		
/	Supreme Military Majlis ul-Shura of the United Mujahideen Forces of the Caucasus				X	
61.	Taliban				X	
/	Tamil Nadu Liberation Army			X		

		AUSTRALIA	EU	INDIA	RUSSIA	US
/	Tamil National Retrieval Troops			X		
/	Tehrik-e Taliban Pakistan					X
62.	Ulster Defence Association (UDA) / Ulster Freedom Fighters (UFF)		X			
63.	United Liberation Front of Assam (ULFA)			X		
64.	United National Liberation Front (UNLF)			X		
65.	United Self-Defence Forces of Colombia (AUC)		X			X

Designated Organization:

United States of America
30

Colombia
48, 56, 65

Peru
60

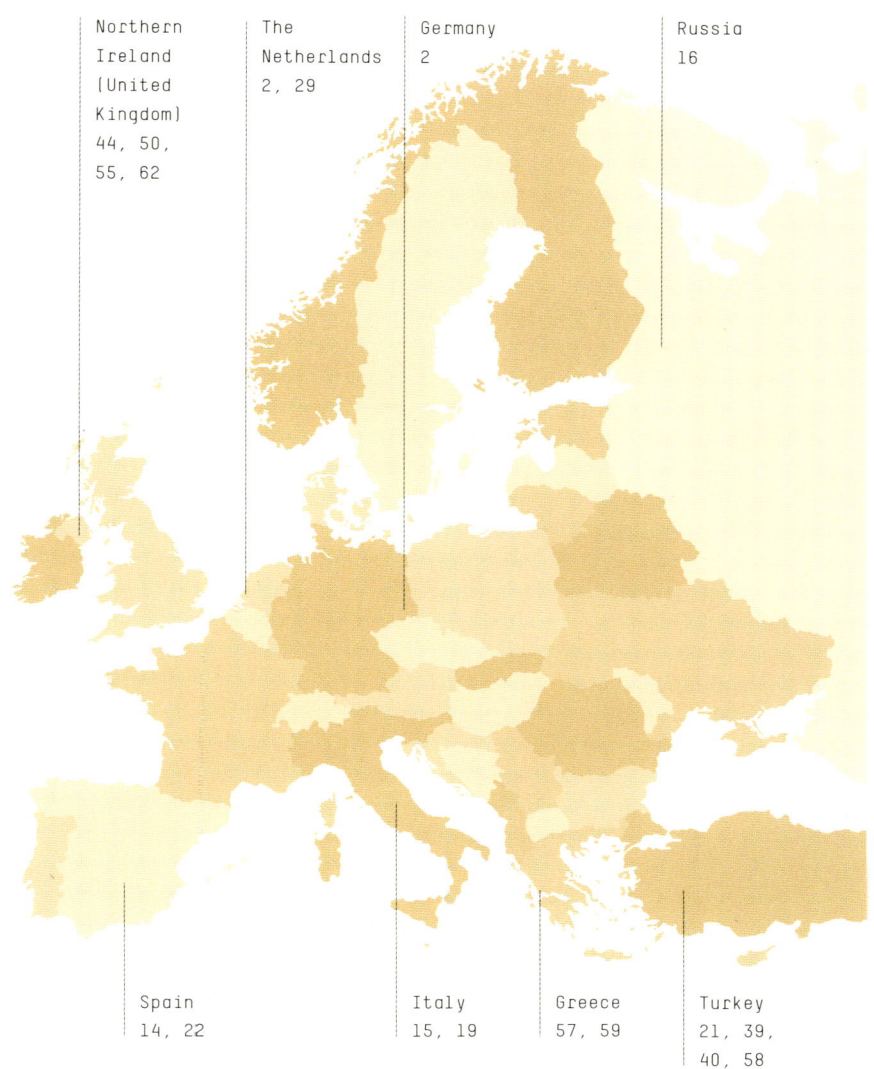

Northern
Ireland
(United
Kingdom)
44, 50,
55, 62

The
Netherlands
2, 29

Germany
2

Russia
16

Spain
14, 22

Italy
15, 19

Greece
57, 59

Turkey
21, 39,
40, 58

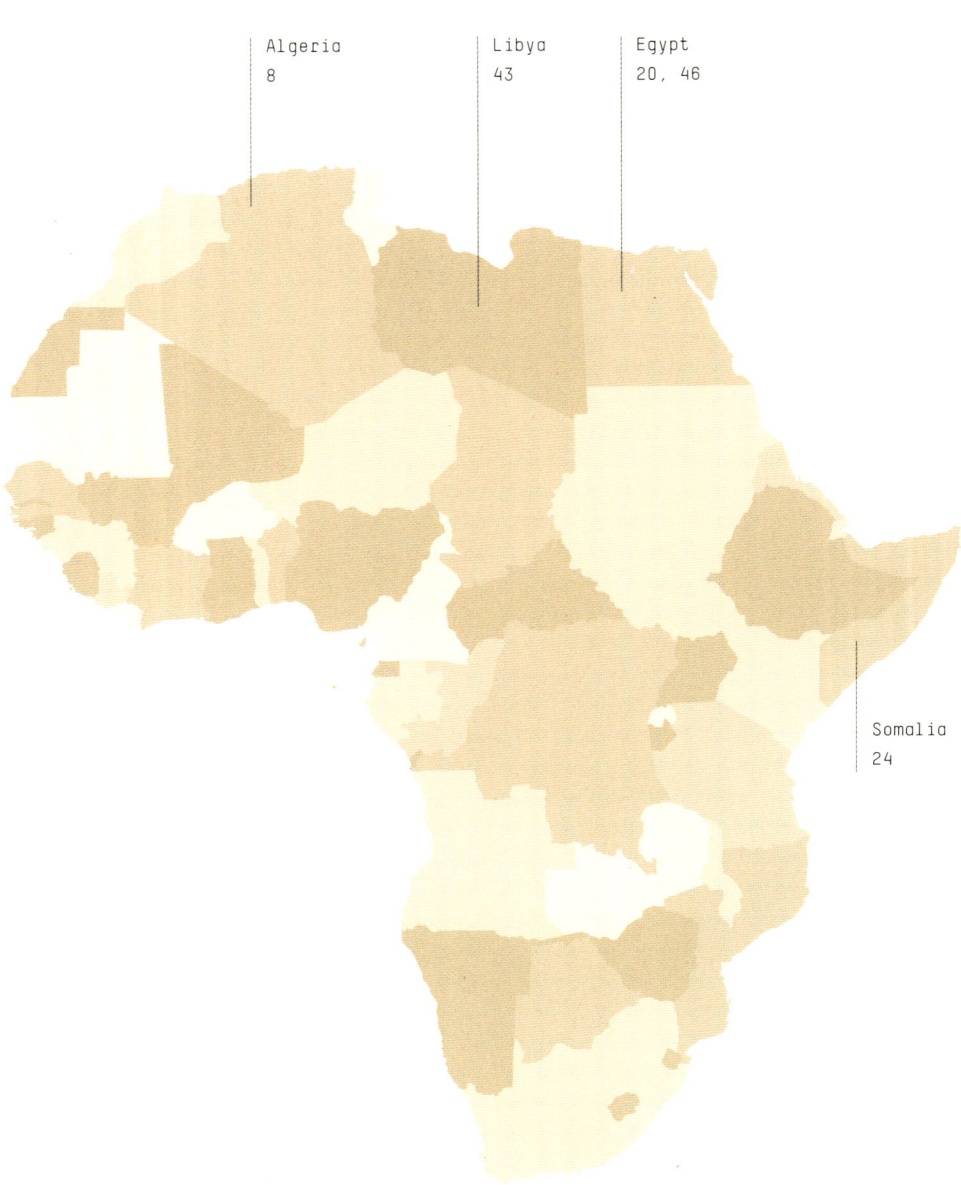

Algeria
8

Libya
43

Egypt
20, 46

Somalia
24

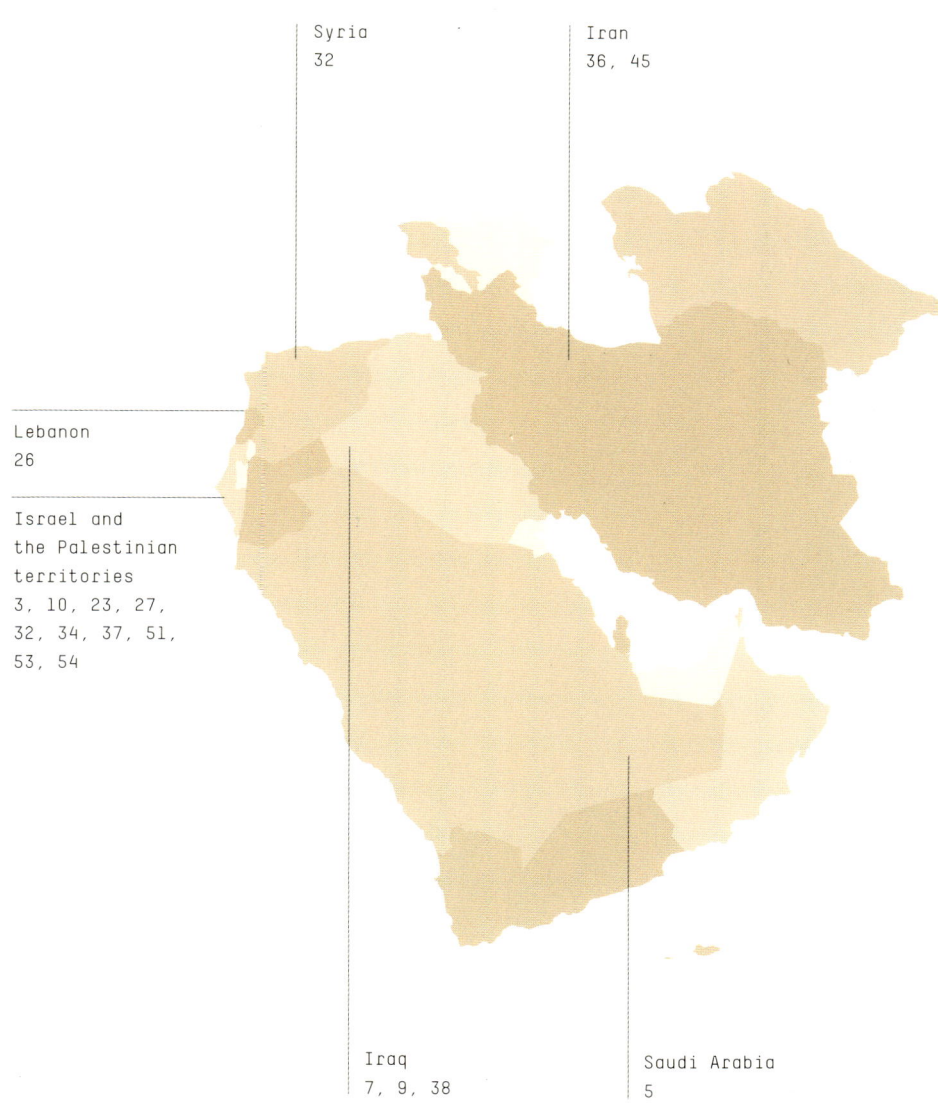

Syria
32

Iran
36, 45

Lebanon
26

Israel and
the Palestinian
territories
3, 10, 23, 27,
32, 34, 37, 51,
53, 54

Iraq
7, 9, 38

Saudi Arabia
5

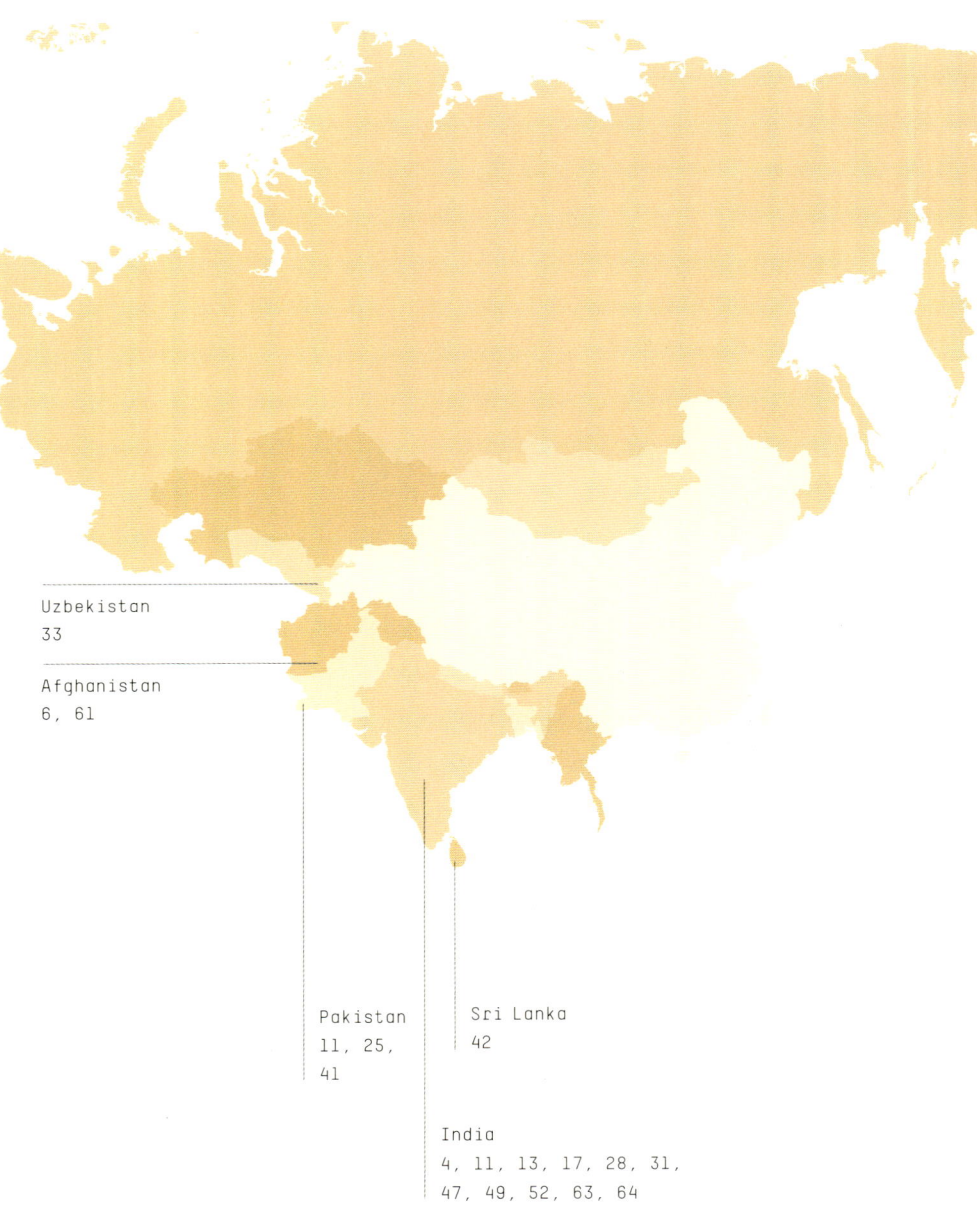

Uzbekistan
33

Afghanistan
6, 61

Pakistan
11, 25,
41

Sri Lanka
42

India
4, 11, 13, 17, 28, 31,
47, 49, 52, 63, 64

Japan
12

Philippines
1, 18

Indonesia
35

1. ABU SAYYAF GROUP (ASG)

Name in Filipino: Grupong Abu Sayyaf

The Abu Sayyaf Group (ASG) was established in the late 1980s by Abdurajik Janjalani (also known as Abu Sayyaf, 'bearer of the sword'), an associate of the founder of »al-Qaeda, Osama bin Laden. Janjalani's goal was to create in the Philippines' predominantly Christian areas of western Mindanao and the Sulu Archipelago an independent Islamic state based on sharia law.

The ASG was initially funded by al-Qaeda, and engaged in acts of political and religious terrorism, such as bombings and killings, against Christian churches and missionaries, and non-Muslim communities. The group lost its ideological leader upon Janjalani's death in a shoot-out with Filipino police in 1998. This, combined with the decreasing finances resulting from the dismantling of the global al-Qaeda network financing scheme by the United States and other Western countries, caused the ASG to disintegrate into factions, which turned to high-profile kidnap for ransom, demanding up to $1 million for each hostage. In 2012 the Philippine government estimated ASG's cadre strength as about 380. The group lacks a clear command-and-control structure, and although its factions are capable of coordinating activities and operations, they tend to act autonomously.

April	1995	ASG operatives attack the western Mindanao town of Ipil, killing 53 people and wounding 48, and burn and loot numerous commercial buildings
April	2000	ASG faction kidnaps 21 people for ransom from a Malaysian resort
February	2004	Bombing of a ferry in Manila Bay, Philippines, killing at least 116 people

Sword   Globe   Open Qur'an   *First part of the shahada:*
'There is no god but God [Allah]'

Second part of the shahada:
'Muhammad is His messenger'

COLOUR	PANTONE CODE	CMYK	RGB
	1797	0.100.99.4	220.8.20
	process yellow	0.0.100.0	255.233.0
	364	65.0.100.42	69.128.31
	process black	0.0.0.100	29.29.27

The globe at the centre of the ASG logo symbolizes the global aspirations of the group. The open Qur'an, and the shahada – the Muslim declaration of faith – on banners above and below it, give religious legitimacy to the ASG's ideology and activities. The sword represents jihad ('struggle'), which is also given religious legitimacy, and serves as a reminder of the violent nature of the ASG's fight to achieve its goals. The fervent aspirations of the group are further symbolized by the colour red, which stands for bloodshed and revolution.

2. AL-AQSA FOUNDATION (AAF)

Name in Arabic: مؤسسة الأقصى

Transliteration: musasa al-aqsa

The al-Aqsa Foundation (AAF; <u>al-Aqsa</u> is the Arabic for 'the farthest') was founded in 1991 as an international charity organization headquartered in Aachen, Germany. Its statute states that its goal is to assist Palestinians around the world, to launch humanitarian projects in the Palestinian territories (the West Bank and the Gaza Strip), and to support and promote educational institutions there. Numerous local branches were established in several European countries, including The Netherlands.

The AAF collected donations in mosques and Islamic cultural centres, and at non-religious meetings, public rallies and demonstrations dedicated to the Middle East conflict. The donated funds were transferred to social and humanitarian organizations in the Palestinian territories that formed part of the organizational structure and environment of the »Hamas movement.

In 2002 a German court ruled that the AAF's German branch, al-Aqsa e.V., actively advocated, provoked and enforced the use of force in support of political, religious and other interests, and that it sustained a group outside the German federal territory that encouraged attacks against people and property. It was ruled that these efforts were directed against the concept of international understanding. The German authorities banned and dissolved the AAF's German branch. The Dutch government followed suit in 2003, listing the group's Dutch branch, Stichting al-Aqsa, as a terrorist organization.

Olive-tree
branches on left
and right

Name of group in Arabic

AL-AQSA

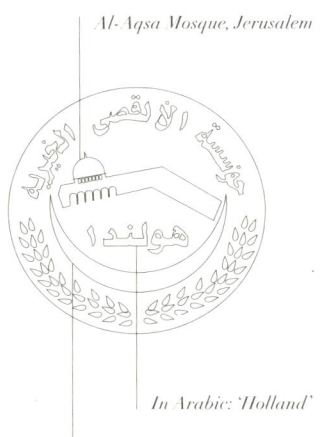

Al-Aqsa Mosque, Jerusalem

In Arabic: 'Holland'

Crescent moon

COLOUR	PANTONE CODE	CMYK	RGB
	0209	0.100.99.4	220.8.20
	104	0.3.100.30	199.180.0
	3425	100.0.78.42	0.105.68
	1788	0.84.88.0	232.68.39
	process black	0.0.0.100	0.0.0

Logo of the AAF

Logo of the AAF's Dutch branch

The various regional Al-Aqsa Foundation logos feature common elements. The name of the group is written in Arabic in a semicircle. Two connected branches of an olive tree, symbolizing the group's peaceful ambitions and actions, close the circle; the crescent moon just above them is a symbol of Islamic identity and, coloured in red, serves as the emblem of a humanitarian organization, similar to the Red Cross. The Al-Aqsa Mosque in Jerusalem, used as an Islamic image of Palestinian national identity, straddles the centre of the logo. The name of the country in which the branch is located is displayed in red between the mosque and the crescent.

3. AL-AQSA MARTYRS BRIGADES (AAMB)

Name in Arabic: كتائب شهداء الأقصى

Transliteration: kata:b shahida al-aqsa

The al-Aqsa Martyrs Brigades (AAMB) emerged in the Palestinian
territories in 2000 as a militia loyal to Fatah, the secular nationalist
movement led by Yasser Arafat (1929-2004). The group was reportedly
founded by young officers from Arafat's security services and the
leader of Tanzim, one of Fatah's militant factions, Marwan Barghouti.

Ideologically, the AAMB is focused on Palestinian nationalism, not
political Islam. The group accepts the existence of the Israeli state
but seeks an end to Israel's presence in the Palestinian territories
(the West Bank and the Gaza Strip). It has engaged in guerrilla warfare
against Israeli military forces and settlers in the West Bank, with
operations including roadside ambushes, drive-by shootings and car
bombings. It came as a surprise to international observers when in
2002 the AAMB began targeting civilians inside Israel with suicide
bombings, a tactic predominantly used by Islamist groups.

In June 2007, Fatah-opposed »Hamas took control of the Gaza Strip;
as a consequence, numerous AAMB members were arrested or killed. The
AAMB still exists, but its activity has greatly diminished.

January	2002	The AAMB claims the first female suicide bombing inside Israel, in a shopping street in Jerusalem, killing 1 person and injuring 100 others
January	2003	Double suicide bombing in downtown Tel Aviv, Israel, killing 23 people and injuring more than 100
January	2008	AAMB joins Hamas and Palestinian Islamic Jihad to fire rockets into Israel from the Gaza Strip

In Arabic, from the Qur'an (9:14): 'Fight against them so that
Allah will punish them by your hands and disgrace them and give
you victory over them and heal the breasts of a believing people'

Hand grenade

Crossed M16 assault rifles

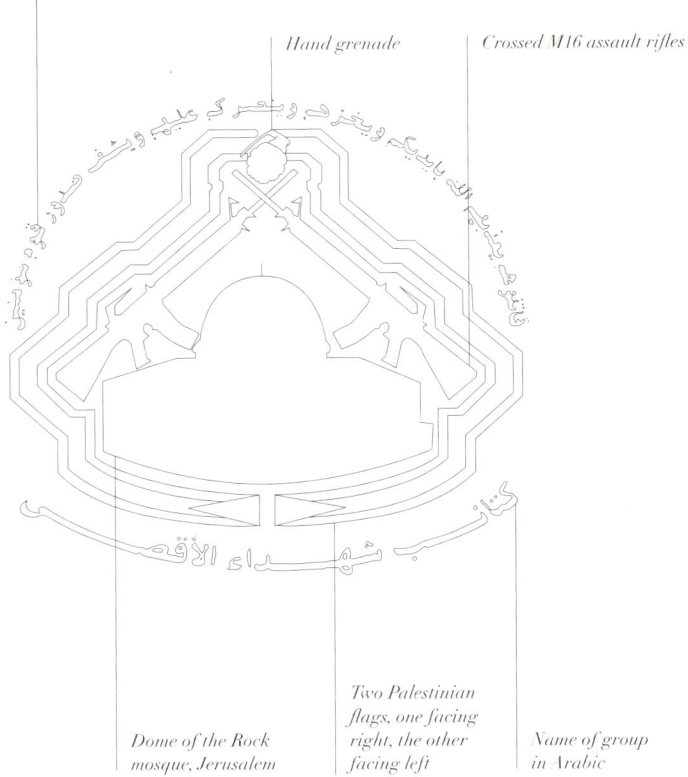

Dome of the Rock
mosque, Jerusalem

Two Palestinian
flags, one facing
right, the other
facing left

Name of group
in Arabic

COLOUR	PANTONE CODE	CMYK	RGB
	186	0.100.81.4	221.5.43
	356	95.0.100.27	0.125.50
	process black	0.0.0.100	29.29.27

In the centre of the AAMB logo is the Dome of the Rock mosque in Jerusalem, stated by many Islamic scholars to be the site from which the Prophet Muhammad ascended to Heaven (others name the site of his ascension as the nearby Al-Aqsa Mosque), making it one of the holiest sites in Islam. Here, the Dome of the Rock is used as a Palestinian national symbol. In combination with the two crossed M16 assault rifles and the hand grenade, it highlights the group's willingness to use armed struggle to reclaim the holy site and the land of Palestine. Two elongated Palestinian flags encircle the entire image, further signifying the group's objective of establishing a Palestinian state. The Qur'anic verse at the top legitimizes the group's actions. The logo thus evokes both national duty and religious sacrifice.

4. AL-BADR (AB)

Name in Arabic: البدر

There have been several Islamic militant groups with the name al-Badr (AB), a reference to the Prophet Muhammad's victory at the Battle of Badr (see p. 43). The most recent emerged in 1998. The group's stated goal is to remove the Indian state of Jammu and Kashmir from that country's control and to integrate it with Pakistan. It also advocates the spread of Islam over South Asia and the strict adherence to Islamic doctrine and sharia law in daily life. According to the Indian government, AB is closely tied to one of Pakistan's three intelligence agencies, the Inter-Services Intelligence (ISI).

Indian security forces estimate that AB has 300 fighters, two-thirds of them Pakistanis who have received training in Afghanistan and in Pakistan's Waziristan region; the remainder are foreign mercenaries. The group employs explosives and suicide squads to carry out its operations, and its targets have included representatives of the Indian government and military. It has consistently been opposed to any sort of dialogue between India and Pakistan, and has urged Pakistan to 'concentrate upon strengthening jihad instead of wasting further time seeking a negotiated settlement'.

December	2002	Shooting in the village of Hasiot in the Jammu region of India, killing 5 civilians
February	2005	Attack on Jammu and Kashmir's administrative offices in Srinagar, India; 2 perpetrators and 5 others are killed
April	2008	Abduction in Kashmir's Kupwara district of 2 police constables, who are found dead the next day

The shahada: 'There is no god but God [Allah],
and Muhammad is His messenger'

Sword

Name of group in Arabic

COLOUR	PANTONE CODE	CMYK	RGB
	process black	0.0.0.100	0.0.0

The group's name, al-Badr, is a direct reference to the Battle of Badr (AD 624) fought by the Prophet Muhammad and his supporters against opponents based in Mecca, now in modern-day Saudi Arabia. The battle, one of the few to be explicitly mentioned in the Qur'an (3:123-25), was a turning point in Muhammad's struggle against perceived unbelievers, and his decisive victory is attributed to divine intervention. The name 'al-Badr' evokes notions of the divine. The flag used by the group features the shahada, the Muslim declaration of faith, emphasizing adherence to Islamic ideology. The sword, a pre-modern weapon, symbolizes violent struggle and links the group's campaign to early Islamic history.

5. AL-HARAMAIN ISLAMIC FOUNDATION (HIF)

Name in Arabic: مؤسسة الحرمين الخيرية

The al-Haramain Islamic Foundation (HIF; <u>al-Haramain</u> is Arabic for 'the holy'), officially listed by the Russian Federation as the al-Haramain Foundation, is an organization headquartered in Saudi Arabia, with branches and local intermediaries in North America, Europe, Asia and Africa. It describes itself as a private charitable and educational organization dedicated to promoting greater understanding of Islam and its teachings throughout the world. The group's activities include engaging in charitable activities, operating prayer houses and distributing religious publications. It is funded by grants from various countries and by donations from private businesses. In 2011 the US District Court for the District of Oregon stated that the HIF's Saudi Arabian branch had an annual budget of \$30–\$80 million.

According to evidence provided by the Oregon district court, HIF field offices and representatives have provided financial, logistical, technological and material support to terrorist organizations affiliated to the ›al-Qaeda network, such as »Hamas and »Lashkar-e-Tayyiba. In 2004 the US Treasury alleged that the group's American branch had engaged in money laundering and, as quoted from the book <u>Dirty Dealing</u> (2006) by Peter Lilley, in concealing the movement of funds intended for fighters in Chechnya to support their jihad against the Russian authorities.

December	2000	The HIF American branch, based in Oregon, donates \$150,000 to HIF Saudi Arabia for humanitarian purposes in Chechnya
June	2004	The US Treasury bans the HIF American branch

Name of group in Arabic

In Arabic, the word **dawa**: 'to summon',
'to invite', in the sense of 'to call for prayer'

Sun

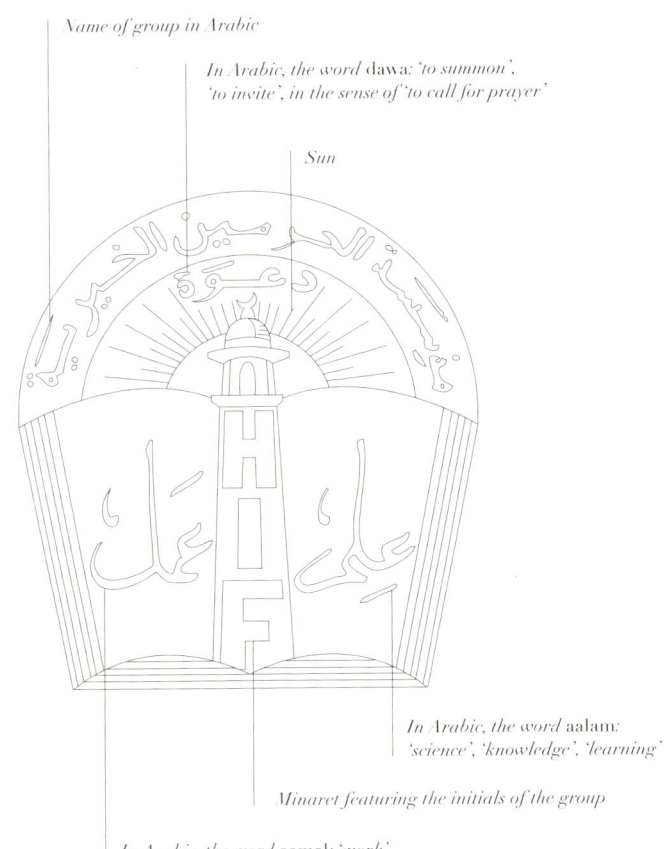

In Arabic, the word **aalam**:
'science', 'knowledge', 'learning'

Minaret featuring the initials of the group

In Arabic, the word **aamal**: 'work'

COLOUR	PANTONE CODE	CMYK	RGB
	3305	100.0.61.61	0.82.67
	110	0.12.100.7	244.207.0
	1807	0.100.96.28	178.14.16
	271	43.37.0.0	159.160.208

The elements used in the HIF logo symbolize the organization's Islamic identity. A minaret (usually a part of a mosque) bearing the group's initials emerges from a book representing the Qur'an; this evokes notions of the divine, and associates the HIF and its work with Allah (God), conferring spiritual and religious legitimacy. Above the minaret is the Arabic word dawa ('to summon' or 'to invite'), most widely used in the sense of 'to call for prayer'. The concept of dawa relates to understanding Islam through a process of dialogue, thus symbolizing HIF's aims of promoting greater understanding of Islam. Positioning the word within the rays of the sun associates it with the divine. On the pages of the book are the words aalam ('knowledge', 'science' or 'learning') and aamal ('work'), both of which are part of the philosophy the organization wants to project: learning and working are integral to a meaningful Islamic life.

6. AL-QAEDA (AQ)

Name in Arabic: القاعدة

Al-Qaeda (Arabic for 'the base'; AQ) was formed in Afghanistan in about 1988 as a network of militant Islamist fighters. Its founders were the Palestinian Islamic theologian Abdullah Azzam and the Saudi Arabian Osama bin Laden; their idea was to assimilate mujahideen (Islamic guerrilla fighters) who had come from more than fifty countries to fight the Soviet invasion of Afghanistan in 1979, and to continue the 'holy war' beyond that country's borders. The holy war aims to rid Muslim countries of the cultural and political influence of Western countries, and to replace their governments with fundamentalist Islamic regimes based on rigid sharia law. Over time, AQ has evolved into an international network of terrorists and associated organizations with immense ideological and financial influence.

The AQ network is administered by a council that discusses and approves major undertakings, including terrorist operations. After Bin Laden was killed in 2011 by an American special forces unit, his former deputy and AQ's ideological adviser, Ayman al-Zawahiri, an Egyptian physician and Islamic theologian, took over the leadership.

August	1998	Near-simultaneous bombings at American embassies in Nairobi, Kenya, and Dar es Salaam, Tanzania, killing 222 people and injuring more than 4000
September	2001	Suicide hijacking of 4 American domestic flights: 2 planes crash into the World Trade Center in New York, 1 into the side of the Pentagon (Department of Defense) in Virginia, and 1 in a field in Pennsylvania. In total, 2985 people are recorded as having died in the attacks
July	2005	Suicide bombings in London - 3 on the London Underground and 1 on a bus - killing 56 people and injuring more than 700

The shahada: 'There is no god but God [Allah], and Muhammad is His messenger'

COLOUR	PANTONE CODE	CMYK	RGB
■	process black	0.0.0.100	0.0.0

The black flag associated with al-Qaeda is the black flag referred to in Arabic as a̱l-raya and commonly dubbed the 'Flag of Jihad'. It has been a symbol of religious revolt and battle since the founding of Islam in the seventh century: the Prophet Muhammad and many of his companions are said to have carried a similar black flag into battle. It gained prominence in 2011, after al-Qaeda's hijacking of aeroplanes in the Jnited States and the destruction of the World Trade Center in New York, and is now used by numerous groups worldwide. Its use emphasizes the importance and occurrence of jihad (war against unbelievers) today, and evokes sentiments rooted in the desire to establish a Sunni caliphate. In Islam, the colour black further symbolizes religious adherence and strict Islamic piety.

7. AL-QAEDA IN IRAQ (AQI)

Name in Arabic: القاعدة في العراق

Transliteration: al-qaedah fi iraq

The Jordanian militant Islamist Abu Musab al-Zarqawi founded the group in 2003 as a reaction to the US-led invasion and occupation of Iraq that led to the fall of the country's ruler, Saddam Hussein. Al-Zarqawi initially joined forces with the Islamic Kurdish group »Ansar al-Islam under the name Jama'at al-Tawhid wa'al-Jihad ('group of monotheism and jihad'). In 2004 the group was renamed the al-Qaeda Jihad Organization in the Land of Two Rivers, more commonly referred to as al-Qaeda in Iraq (AQI). Now the largest and most active Sunni militant outfit in Iraq, AQI has an estimated cadre strength of 2000-4000, and AQI members form the majority of the Sunni umbrella organization the Islamic State of Iraq (founded in 2006).

The primary religious, political and ideological aims of AQI are to expel foreign forces from Iraq, and to establish an Islamic caliphate based on sharia law in Iraq and ultimately throughout the region. Since the withdrawal of most US troops in late 2011, AQI has focused on targeting the Iraqi government, which is mainly Shiite, and the Shia population. The group carries out suicide, car and roadside bombings, shootings, assassinations, abductions and paramilitary operations.

November	2006	Series of car bombs and mortar attacks in Sadr City, a suburb of Baghdad, killing 202 people and injuring at least 250
August	2007	Truck bombs in 2 villages near Sinjar, northern Iraq, killing 500 people and injuring 1500
December	2009	Several explosions near government buildings in Baghdad, killing 130 people and injuring at least 400

Open book (probably
representing the Qur'an)

Rifle and fist with index
finger extended

Flag

In Arabic, part
of the group's
name: 'Monotheism
and Jihad'

Globe

COLOUR	PANTONE CODE	CMYK	RGB
	113	0.7.66.0	255.231.111
	process black	0.0.0.100	0.0.0

This was the logo of Jama'at al-Tawhid wa'al-Jihad, the group now known
as al-Qaeda in Iraq. The black background refers to the black battle
flag of the Prophet Muhammad (see p. 51), evoking militancy and jihad
and representing the goal of establishing a Sunni caliphate. The
globe represents the group's worldwide ambitions, while the book –
most likely symbolizing the Qur'an – signifies the group's ideological
foundation in Islam. Above the book rise an assault rifle (a reminder
of the violent nature of jihad), a flag and a fist with the index
finger pointing up to God, legitimizing the militant struggle. The
yellow Arabic writing at the bottom ('Monotheism and Jihad') gives
part of the group's name, but also serves as a slogan.

*Three outstretched arms holding
a black flag featuring the shahada:
'There is no god but God [Allah], and
Muhammad is His messenger'*

Border

COLOUR	PANTONE CODE	CMYK	RGB
	113	0.7.66.0	255.231.111
	473	0.23.36.0	252.209.171
	7456	55.35.0.7	123.147.197
	process black	0.0.0.100	0.0.0

The three outstretched arms in the logo of al-Qaeda in Iraq represent
the unification of the country's various militant Sunni organizations
under one banner. They evoke a mountain-like image that symbolizes
the mountainous region of northern Iraq, where the organization was
established. The flag is a reference to the black battle flag of the
Prophet Muhammad (see p. 51), while the shahada, the Muslim declaration
of faith, signifies the group's ideological foundation in Islam.

The shahada: 'There is no god but God [Allah], and Muhammad is His messenger'

Circle representing the full moon

COLOUR	PANTONE CODE	CMYK	RGB
	process yellow	0.0.100.0	255.237.0
	process black	0.0.0.100	0.0.0

Jama'at al-Tawhid wa'al-Jihad, the group now known as al-Qaeda in Iraq, used this flag in 2003 and 2004, in videos in which the group beheaded hostages. The shahada (the Muslim declaration of faith) runs along the top of the flag, representing the group's ideological foundation in Islam. The circle beneath it represents the full moon, symbolizing the power of God. The name of the group was usually displayed either above or underneath the moon.

Second part of the shahada:
'Muhammad is His messenger'

COLOUR	PANTONE CODE	CMYK	RGB
■	process black	0.0.0.100	0.0.0

This is the flag of the Sunni Islamist umbrella organization the Islamic State of Iraq (ISI), which is composed largely of members of al-Qaeda in Iraq. In a document entitled 'The Legality of the Flag in Islam', issued by the organization in 2007, the ISI states that the black battle flag used by the Prophet Muhammad (see p. 51) was square. Most Islamic scholars agree that Muhammad used a piece of black velvet owned by one of his wives, Aisha, to create the banner.

The ISI's flag features the shahada, the Muslim declaration of faith. The first part runs along the top, and the seal below contains the second part. The ISI's document contains evidence and legitimacy for the design from Islamic scholars, who state that the seal is an accurate representation of the one used by Muhammad in his letters to foreign leaders. The words are written in reverse order, reading from top to bottom 'Allah', 'Messenger' and, finally, 'Muhammad'.

8. AL-QAEDA IN THE ISLAMIC MAGHREB (AQIM)

Name in Arabic: تنظيم القاعدة في بلاد المغرب الإسلامي

Transliteration: tanzim al-qaedah fi bilad al-maghrib al-islami

Al-Qaeda in the Islamic Maghreb (AQIM) is a Sunni Islamist militant organization that evolved from the Algerian Sunni militant group Salafist Group for Call and Combat (better known by its French-language initials, GSPC). The GSPC was formed in 1998 and was locally focused, concentrating on fighting the secular Algerian military government. In 2006 »al-Qaeda's number two, Ayman al-Zawahiri, announced a 'blessed union' between AQIM and al-Qaeda, and AQIM has since pursued wider goals under the banner of 'global jihad'. Its several hundred fighters remain regionally focused in their operations, however, with aspirations of overthrowing 'apostate' African regimes (those who have rejected Islam) and creating an Islamic caliphate.

Compared to the GSPC, AQIM's rhetoric is more anti-Western, and the group has called for jihadis everywhere to target Jews, Christians and apostates. Its broader aim is to fight American and French interests in order to end their representation in Algeria. The group employs conventional terrorist tactics, including guerrilla-style ambushes against military personnel and truck bombings against government targets, but relies predominantly on suicide attacks. It also engages in kidnappings of Westerners, either for ransom in order to finance its operations or as a bargaining point in negotiating the release of imprisoned Islamic militants.

February	2003	GSPC militants kidnap 32 European tourists travelling in the Algerian Sahara, and receive an estimated $5-$10 million ransom
September	2007	A suicide bomber attempts to assassinate the Algerian president, Abdelaziz Bouteflika, killing 22 people and injuring 107
December	2007	Double suicide bombing in Algiers, killing 41 people, including 17 United Nations staff members, and injuring some 175

In Arabic, from the Qur'an (2:193): 'And fight them until there is no more disbelief and worship is for Allah alone'

AK-47 assault rifle with attached flag featuring the shahada ('There is no god but God [Allah], and Muhammad is His messenger')

In Arabic, from the Qur'an (6:57): 'The command rests with none but Allah'

Sun with seven rays

Olive-tree branches on right and left

Sword

In Arabic on white 'path': al Sunna (the collected teachings of the Prophet Muhammad)

Grey brick wall

Name of group in Arabic

COLOUR	PANTONE CODE	CMYK	RGB
	348	100.0.85.24	0.126.72
	311	63.0.12.0	82.193.221
	471	0.59.100.18	207.112.0
	7510	0.30.72.11	230.175.82
	process black	0.0.0.100	0.0.0

The logo of the Salafist Group for Call and Combat, the predecessor of al-Qaeda in the Islamic Maghreb, has as its centrepiece the Qur'an and, in the 'path' leading up to it, a reference to the Sunna (the collected teachings of the Prophet Muhammad), signifying the group's ideological grounding and its strong devotion to Allah (God), Muhammad and Islam. This is reinforced by the shahada, the Muslim declaration of faith, on the green banner fluttering in front of the sunrays. The sun emphasizes the divine powers associated with the Qur'an. The group's objective of establishing a Sunni caliphate guided by sharia law is illustrated by the quotation from the Qur'an running in a semicircle at the top. The sword references the early jihad of Muhammad, while the assault rifle represents contemporary jihad. The phrase shown on the Qur'an legitimizes jihad. The wall in the bottom half stands for strong foundations, while the olive-tree branches on each side symbolize prosperity.

AK-47
assault rifle

Black flag featuring the shahada:
'There is no god but God [Allah],
and Muhammad is His messenger'

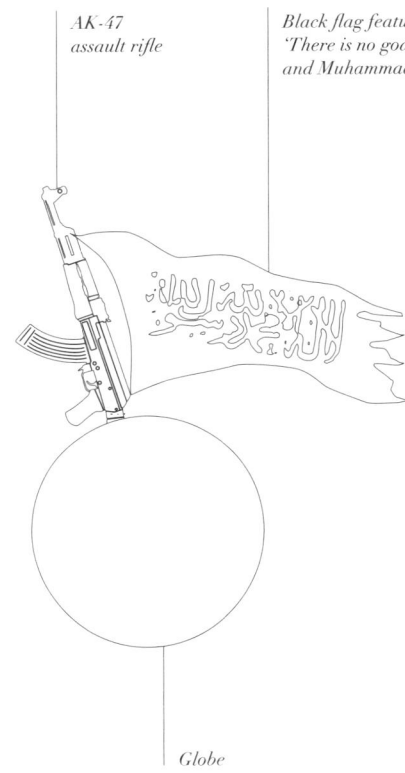

Globe

COLOUR	PANTONE CODE	CMYK	RGB
	1817	0.90.100.66	109.27.0
	process black	0.0.0.100	0.0.0

Branding Terror   *066*

The globe in the logo of al-Qaeda in the Islamic Maghreb represents the group's aim of establishing a worldwide Islamic caliphate; the black flag, based on the battle flag of the Prophet Muhammad (see p. 51), represents this caliphate and connects the current jihad struggle to the jihad of early Islam. The shahada, the Muslim declaration of faith, symbolizes the group's devotion to Islamic ideals. The AK-47 assault rifle symbolizes militancy, which the group is ready to employ in order to achieve its aims.

9. ANSAR AL-ISLAM (AAI)

Name in Arabic: أنصار الإسلام

Ansar al-Islam (Arabic for 'supporters of Islam'; AAI) was formed in 2001 as an umbrella organization for Sunni extremist groups within the Kurdish Autonomous Zone (KAZ) in northern Iraq. Its objective is to overthrow the secular Kurdish leadership and establish an independent Islamic state in the KAZ.

The organization has evolved over the years, operating under multiple names. In a statement released in 2003, AAI members called upon all jihadists in Iraq to unite under the name Ansar al-Sunna ('supporters of the Sunna', the collected teachings of the Prophet Muhammad; AAS). Following this statement, attacks conducted by AAI were claimed under the name of AAS. The group has targeted members of the Iraqi government, police and military forces, as well as Iraqi infrastructure, with suicide attacks, car bombings and shootings. It has also conducted hostage-takings, executions and targeted assassinations.

In 2007 several high-level figures were reported to have left AAS owing to the organization's links to the group »al-Qaeda in Iraq, which was accused of having killed AAS members. That same year, AAS reverted to its original name of AAI. In 2011 AAI released a statement announcing the creation of new flags (shown on p. 71).

February	2004	Simultaneous attacks on offices of the political parties Patriotic Union of Kurdistan and Kurdistan Democratic Party in Irbil, Iraq, killing 105 people and injuring 130
August	2004	Release of a video showing 12 Nepalese hostages being executed for 'serving the Jews and the Christians' and 'believing in Buddha as their god'
May	2007	Suicide car-bomb attack on the headquarters of the Kurdish Democratic Party, killing at least 30 people and injuring 115

The shahada: 'There is no god but God [Allah],
and Muhammad is His messenger'

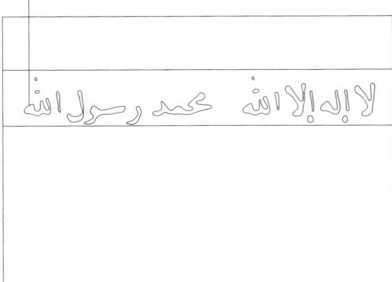

COLOUR	PANTONE CODE	CMYK	RGB
■	process black	0.0.0.100	0.0.0

Command flag of AAI

*Flag of AAI's
Military and Jihad Department*

The two versions of the AAI flag are similar, but with the colours reversed. The colour black is used as a reference to both the battle flag of the Prophet Muhammad (see p. 51) and the Abbasid Caliphate (750-1258), which had its capital in Baghdad and used a plain black flag. Black thus evokes a historical sense of jihad, represents the contemporary concept of the struggle, and emphasizes its importance. It also symbolizes religious adherence and strict piety. Running across the flag is the shahada, the Muslim declaration of faith, reinforcing the group's devotion to Islam. White symbolizes purity, piety and religious authority. The white-background flag gives religious legitimacy to the work of the AAI's Military and Jihad Department, and communicates the religious duty to conduct jihad.

10. ARMY OF ISLAM (AOI)

Name in Arabic: جيش الإسلام
Transliteration: jaish al-islam

Army of Islam (AOI), also known by its Arabic name, Jaish al-Islam, and as the Tawhid and Jihad Brigades, is a Palestinian group based in the Gaza Strip. It was founded in 2005 and numbers several hundred members. Its ideology is based on Salafist ideas promoting global jihad coupled with the traditional model of armed Palestinian resistance against perceived Israeli occupation. The AOI has expressed its affiliation with and support of »al-Qaeda. It is linked to the radical cleric Abu Qatada, a Palestinian of Jordanian citizenship who has been referred to as al-Qaeda's spiritual leader in Europe. Qatada was convicted in his absence of terrorism charges in Jordan in 1999; at the time of going to press he was living in the United Kingdom, where he was fighting government attempts to extradite him to Jordan.

The group targets what in a video it called 'the US and its allies' and the 'children of monkeys and pigs' (an Islamic anti-Semitic reference to Jews, taken from the Qur'an). The AOI became widely known in 2006 after it captured Israeli soldier Gilad Shalit and then turned him over to »Hamas. The group has abducted other Israeli soldiers, foreign aid workers and journalists, has launched mortar and rocket attacks into Israel, and has allegedly recruited people responsible for various bombings in Egypt.

June	2006	Abduction of Israeli soldier Gilad Shalit, in cooperation with the »Izz ad-Din al-Qassam Brigades; he is released in 2011 as part of a prisoner-exchange deal
March	2007	Abduction of the BBC journalist Alan Johnston; he is released some 4 months later after intervention by »Hamas
January	2011	Bomb attack on a Coptic church in Alexandria, Egypt, killing 25 people and injuring approximately 90

Globe

Sword with black flag attached
featuring the shahada: 'There
is no god but God [Allah], and
Muhammad is His messenger'

Open Qur'an

Name of group in Arabic

COLOUR	PANTONE CODE	CMYK	RGB
	113	0.7.66.0	255.231.111
	175	0.65.100.70	125.62.0
	process black	0.0.0.100	0.0.0

The open book at the centre of the AOI logo is the Qur'an, which
emphasizes the origin of the group's ideology and its devotion to
Islam. This is reinforced by the shahada (the Muslim declaration
of faith) on the banner at the top of the image. The globe between
the two stands for the group's aspirations, inspired by the Salafist
ideology of 'global jihad'. The sword is a reminder of the violent
nature of jihad and, as a pre-modern weapon, refers to the early
days of the struggle. Furthermore, the black background is a direct
reference to the battle flag used by the Prophet Muhammad (see p. 51).
The group's name runs along the bottom.

11. ARMY OF MUHAMMAD (JEM)

Name in Urdu: جیش محمد

Transliteration: jaish-e-muhammad

The Army of Muhammad (also known by its initials in Urdu, JEM) is a Sunni extremist group based in Pakistan. Founded in 2000 and currently led by Masood Azhar, the former leader of the Islamic militant organization Harakat al-Ansar (see »Harakat ul-Mujahideen), JEM's primary aim is to 'liberate' Indian-administered Kashmir and unite it with Pakistan under sharia law. Moreover, JEM has expressed the intention of destroying the United States and India, and of unifying the various Kashmiri militant groups in order to achieve its aims. The group is politically aligned with the radical Pakistani political party Jamiat-e Ulema-e-Islam, Fazlur Rehman faction (JUI-F).

Based in the Pakistani towns of Peshawar and Muzaffarabad, JEM has conducted operations in Kashmir, Bangladesh and Afghanistan. Its several hundred armed supporters and thousands of followers are predominantly Pakistani and Kashmiri, but it also has support from Afghans and Arab veterans who fought in Afghanistan, either against the Soviet army or the American and Afghan government forces. It carries out attacks against Indian interests in Kashmir, the secular government of Pakistan and sectarian minorities, using light and heavy machine guns, assault rifles, mortars, improvised explosive devices and rocket-propelled grenades.

October	2001	Suicide attack on the legislative assembly building in Srinagar, in the Indian state of Jammu and Kashmir, killing 31 people
December	2001	Suicide attack on the Indian parliament in New Delhi, in concert with »Lashkar-e-Tayyiba, killing 9 people and injuring 18
July	2008	Killing of 47 Indian troops in the state of Jammu and Kashmir

Vertical bands

Arabic word that can be read as either al-jihad *('the struggle') or* Akbar *('Greatest')*

COLOUR	PANTONE CODE	CMYK	RGB
■	process black	0.0.0.100	0.0.0

The black-and-white banner of JEM features a black circle at its centre, a reminder of the Prophet Muhammad's battle flag (see p. 51), evokes notions of death and militancy. The word in the black circle can be read as either <u>al-jihad</u> ('the struggle'), a reference to the concept of jihac as a religious war in the mission of Muhammad against those who are unbelievers, or <u>Akbar</u> ('Greatest'), one of the ninety-nine names for Allah (God) in Islamic tradition. The three vertical stripes are adopted directly from the flag of the Indian-administered state o⁼ Jammu and Kashmir; they represent both the area in which JEM operates and the three regions in the state – Jammu, the Kashmir valley and Lᴊdakh.

12. AUM SHINRIKYO (AUM)

Name in Japanese (Kanji script): オウム真理教

Aum Shinrikyo (Japanese for 'supreme truth'; commonly referred to as Aum) is a religious cult founded in Japan in 1984 by Shoko Asahara, a partially blind guru who claimed to be the first 'enlightened one' since Buddha. Asahara remained Aum's leader until he was sentenced to death in 2004 for masterminding crimes leading to mass deaths (at the time of going to press, his execution had yet to be carried out). His teachings mix Buddhism, Hinduism, Christianity, New Age spirituality and prophecies by the sixteenth-century French apothecary Nostradamus. Asahara preached that the end of the world was near and that Aum followers would be the only people to survive the Apocalypse, and predicted that the United States would hasten Armageddon by starting a nuclear war with Japan. The group's membership was made up mostly of university students from elite families, and was estimated at 1500-2000. In 1990 Aum began assembling a militia with the aim of committing violent attacks in order to accelerate the coming Apocalypse; its team of approximately 300 scientists went on to produce biological and chemical toxins.

In 2000 the group changed its name to Aleph. It has since moved to distance itself from Aum's goals and doctrine, apologized for its past actions and paid reparation to the victims of the Tokyo sarin attack.

June	**1993**	Aum releases anthrax bacteria from a Tokyo building; fails to infect anyone because the group unknowingly uses a non-lethal, vaccine strain
June	**1994**	Sarin gas attack in Matsumoto, Japan, killing 7 people and harming 144
March	**1995**	Sarin gas attack on Tokyo's subway during morning rush hour, killing 12 people and harming more than 5000

Variation of the symbol for the syllable 'om', contained within rings

宗教団体・アレフ

Dove holding a branch

Name of group in Kanji script (left) and Sanskrit-derived script (right)

COLOUR	PANTONE CODE	CMYK	RGB
	2597	85.100.0.0	82.37.131

Logo of Aum Shinrikyo

宗教団休・アレフ

*Logo used after change
of name to Aleph in 2000*

The logo used by Aum until its rebranding as Aleph in 2000 featured a variation of the symbol for the syllable 'om' in the Tibetan alphabet. This syllable is sacred in Hinduism, Buddhism and other Dharmic religions. The syllable, and therefore the symbol in the Aum logo, represents triads, such as the worlds of earth, atmosphere and heaven, or the powers of action, knowledge and will. Thus, the symbol mystically embodies the essence of the entire universe.

As Aleph, the group chose as its logo a dove in the shape of the Hebrew letter 'aleph', which in Jewish mysticism represents the oneness of God. The dove, which carries a small branch, is a symbol of peace. Both elements symbolize the group's rebranding and its efforts to distance itself from past violent acts.

13. BABBAR KHALSA (BKI)

Name in Punjabi [Gurmukhi script]: ਬੱਬਰ ਖ਼ਾਲਸਾ

Transliteration: beber halsa

Babbar Khalsa (also known as Babbar Khalsa International; BKI), formed in 1978, is one of several militant Sikh organizations active in the Punjab region of India and internationally. (Other active groups in that region incude the International Sikh Youth Federation, formed in 1984 and based in the United Kingdom; and the Khalistan Commando Force and Khalistan Zindabad Force, both formed in 1986.) The groups pursue the goal of an independent state in the Sikh homeland of India's Punjab region, the so-called Khalistan, which declared its independence in 1986.

The Sikh religion was founded in the late fifteenth century by the Hindu guru Nanak Nev; it is monotheistic, and opposes polygamy and the Hindu caste system. In India, Sikhs constitute a community of more than 19 million people, 80 per cent of whom are based in the Punjab region. The demand for a separate Sikh nation dates from the creation of the modern state of Pckistan in 1947 following the partition of India. The movement adopted violent means in 1977, when the religious leader Jarnail Singh Bhindranwale began to preach in support of armed struggle for national liberation. Acts committed by BKI include assassinations, bombings and kidnappings, aimed at Indian officials and facilities as well as other Sikhs and Hindus.

June	1985	Bomb explosion on an Air India flight from Montreal, Canada, to New Delhi, India, killing all 329 passengers; Canadian law enforcement finds BKI responsible
August	1995	Assassination of the Punjab chief minister, Beant Singh, in a suicide-bomb attack at the civil secretariat in Chandigarh, India
May	2005	Bomb explosions in two cinemas in New Delhi during the screening of an Indian film condemned for denigrating the Sikh faith, killing 1 person and injuring some 50 others

Two kirpan
(single-edged
swords or
daggers)

Khanda
(double-edged sword)

Chakram
(throwing disk)

In Punjabi: 'May I die limb by limb,
but never leave the field of battle'

Name of group in Punjabi

Crossed rifles

COLOUR	PANTONE CODE	CMYK	RGB
■	process black	0.0.0.100	0.0.0

Logo of BKI

Variation of the BKI logo

The BKI logo is based on the Khanda, the most important symbol of Sikhism. This Sikh 'coat of arms' consists of three elements: the khanda double-edged sword, which symbolizes knowledge and the creative power of God; two ceremonial single-edged swords or daggers known as kirpans, symbolizing the integration of spiritual and temporal powers, as well as Sikh political and spiritual sovereignty; and a ring, symbolizing both the traditional circular caldron used to prepare food (emphasizing Sikh doctrine advocating the removal of caste barriers and the equality of people) and the eternal nature of God. The ring has also become associated with the chakram, a throwing disk used in battle. On the ring is the group's motto, which reflects the sacrifice and martyrdom required in order to attain its objectives. The logo supplements the Khanda with two crossed rifles representing armed struggle.

14. BASQUE FATHERLAND AND LIBERTY (ETA)

Name in Euskara: Euskadi ta Askatasuna

Basque Fatherland and Liberty (also known as Basque Homeland and Freedom) is usually referred to by its Euskara (Basque-language) acronym, ETA. The group was founded in 1959 with the aim of establishing an independent Basque state, based on Marxist principles, in the traditional 'Basque Country' of northern Spain and south-western France. The principal targets of its assassinations, bombings and kidnappings have been Spanish government officials, politicians, judicial figures, business people, and security and military forces, as well as journalists and tourist infrastructure. Even though many of ETA's bomb attacks have been preceded by a warning message, allowing the evacuation of people before the explosion, the group is blamed for the deaths of at least 829 people during its five-decade-long campaign of violence.

Current estimates by Spanish authorities put ETA's cadre strength at 100-300. The group has not launched an attack since August 2009. In 2011 ETA declared a definitive end to its violent struggle for an independent Basque state, but the Spanish government has not yet made contact with the group or accepted any international offers to mediate in the situation.

December	**1973**	Assassination of the Spanish prime minister, Luis Carrero Blanco
December	**2006**	Car bomb at Madrid's Barajas International Airport, killing 2 people and injuring 19
July	**2009**	Car bomb in Burgos, Spain, injuring more than 60 people

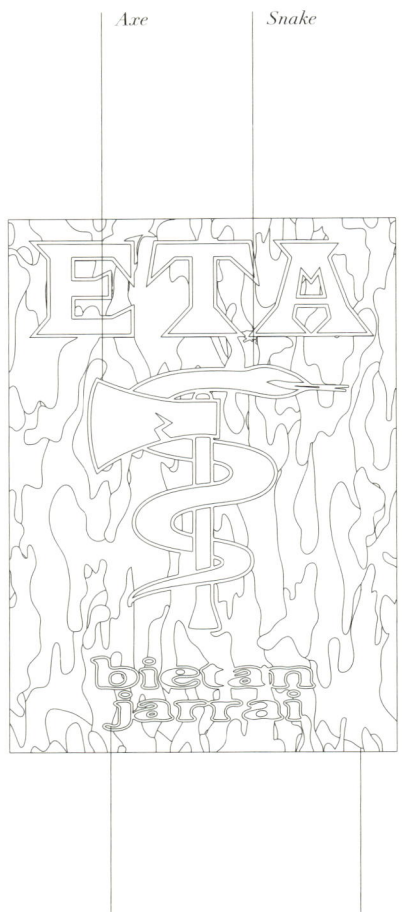

Axe   *Snake*

In Euskara, the group's   *Camouflage background*
motto: 'Keep up on both'   *(optional)*

COLOUR	PANTONE CODE	CMYK	RGB
	2975	30.0.5.0	179.221.235
	292	49.11.0.0	124.182.226
	3145	100.0.19.23	0.113.148
	process black	0.0.0.100	0.0.0

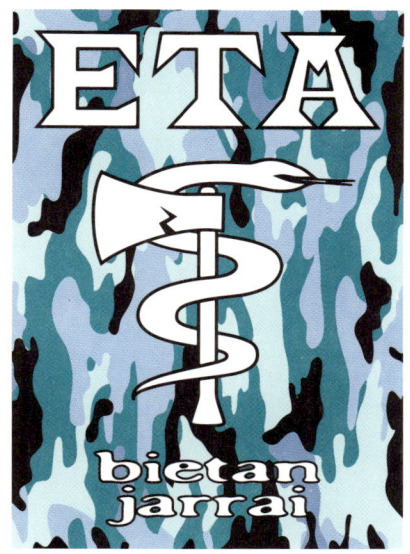

The ETA logo is often seen on murals throughout the Basque Country, or as a flag in the background at ETA press conferences and other events. The axe represents the armed struggle that ETA has been prepared to use in order to achieve its goal of an independent Basque state; the snake represents politics, a second means by which the group has tried to realize its aim. The intertwining of the snake and axe symbolizes the group's belief that politics and armed struggle are inseparable, or that one is the continuation of the other. The motto bietan jarrai at the bottom, written in Euskara, means 'keep up on both', referring to armed struggle and politics. The logo is sometimes given a camouflage background, as in the image above, reinforcing the group's militancy.

15. BRIGATE ROSSE PER LA COSTRUZIONE DEL PARTITO COMUNISTA COMBATTENTE (BR-PCC)

In 1981, arrested members of the radical Italian leftist group Brigate Rosse (the Red Brigades; BR) issued a communiqué calling on their comrades to lay down their arms, stating that 'the international conditions that made this struggle possible no longer exist'. This was the impetus for the creation of a BR splinter group, the Brigate Rosse per la Costruzione del Partito Comunista Combattente (Red Brigades Communist Combatant Party; BR-PCC).

The BR, founded in 1970 and active from 1974 until it suffered mass arrests in the late 1980s, mixed principles of Marxism and Leninism with anarchistic ideas; in particular, it advocated the destruction of the 'imperialist state of multinationals' and the raising of the 'revolutionary consciousness of the working class through acts of armed propaganda'. The group engaged in kidnappings of businessmen, judges, prosecutors and jurors; if ransom money was not paid, the group kneecapped or assassinated its victims. Two separate splinter groups have asserted ownership of the legacy of BR: the BR-PCC, which has claimed responsibility for several assassinations, and the Red Brigades Union of Combatant Communists (BR-UCC), which is less active.

March	1978	BR members kidnap the leader of the Christian Democracy party and former prime minister of Italy, Aldo Moro, killing 5 of his bodyguards in the process; Moro is assassinated 55 days later
May	1999	BR-PCC members assassinate Massimo D'Antona, a senior adviser to the prime minister, Massimo D'Alema
March	2002	BR-PCC members assassinate Marco Biagi, economic adviser to the prime minister, Silvio Berlusconi

COLOUR	PANTONE CODE	CMYK	RGB
▆	process black	0.0.0.100	0.0.0

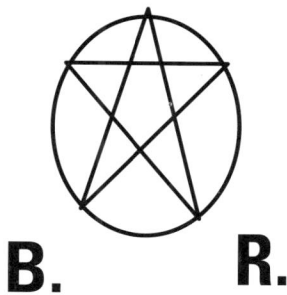

B.   R.

Variations of the BR-PCC logo

The logos of many leftist revolutionary groups contain a five-pointed star, which stands for socialism and (particularly) communism. The BR-PCC uses the same logos as the earlier BR: these feature a pentagram, rather than a solid five-pointed star, so as to differentiate them from the logos of other leftist groups. In communist symbolism, the five-pointed star represents unity. Sometimes the BR star is set on a red background; this is reminiscent of the red flag that symbolizes revolution.

Brigate Rosse per la Costruzione del Partito Comunista Combattente (BR-PCC)

16. CAUCASUS EMIRATE (CE)

Name in Chechen (Cyrillic script): Имарат Кавказ

Transliteration: imarat kavkaz

In 2007 the leader of Chechen Islamist separatists, Doku Umarov, announced the creation of the Caucasus Emirate (CE), an Islamic theocracy based on sharia law. The group, which opposes Russian control of Chechnya, is ideologically guided by a militant interpretation of Salafi Islam infused with ethno-nationalist separatist aspirations.

The CE advocates a reorganization of the North Caucasus in which administrative institutions established by Russia are replaced with a territorially fragmented network of six self-governing vilayets (provinces) to create a multi-ethnic imamate. Territorial armed groups known as jamaats have been formed within each vilayet. Local leaders are appointed by the emir (overall Muslim ruler; currently Umarov himself) and approved by an advisory council, the Majlis al-Shura. Judicial power within the emirate is exercised by a supreme shariat court under the leadership of an Islamic judge, appointed by the emir and approved by the Majlis al-Shura.

The jamaats engage in armed resistance in the name of independence. Actions undertaken by the CE include terrorist attacks in Russia, guerrilla activities within the North Caucasus, and assassinations of officials, such as members of security services, the army and forces of the Russian ministry of the interior.

March	**2010**	Two suicide bombings by 'black widows' (widows of 'martyred' fighters) in Moscow's subway, killing 37 people and injuring 65
October	**2010**	Three militants attack a parliament building in Grozny, Chechnya, killing 3 people and injuring 17 before being killed themselves
January	**2011**	Suicide-bomb attack on Moscow's Domodedovo International Airport, killing 35 people and injuring more than 100

Black oval symbolizing the
al-raya (black battle flag of
the Prophet Muhammad)

The takbir: Allahu akbar
('God is [the] Greatest')

Sabre

Horizontal bands

COLOUR	PANTONE CODE	CMYK	RGB
	1797	0.100.99.4	200.8.20
	348	100.0.85.24	0.126.72
	process black	0.0.0.100	29.29.27

The CE flag is a modified version of the one used by the unrecognized secessionist government of the Chechen Republic of Ichkeria, which was elected in late 1991 and replaced by the CE in 2007. The CE's use of the same colours - green, white and red - as those of its predecessor confirms the group's devotion to historic traditions and its ethno-nationalist separatist ambitions. In Chechen tradition, green is the colour of life; white is associated with the divine, and reflects deep religious devotion and the search for purity; and red symbolizes bloodshed in the struggle for freedom. The CE flag has an added oval al-raya (black battle flag used by the Prophet Muhammad; see p. 51) featuring a horizontal sabre, a reminder of the violent reality of jihadi struggle that links the movement and its aims to early Islam. Inside the oval is the takbir, an Arabic phrase translated as 'God is [the] Greatest'; this is usually used as an informal proclamation of faith, to express celebration or victory in struggle, and to convey determination and defiance in politically charged contexts.

17. COMMUNIST PARTY OF INDIA (MAOIST) (CPI-M)

Name in Hindi: भारतीय कम्युनिस्ट पार्टीर् (माओवादी)

Transliteration: baratki kamyunist parti (maovadi)

In 2004 the two main Indian left-wing extremist groups, the Communist Party of India – Marxist-Leninist People's War and the Maoist Communist Centre of India, merged to form the new organization Communist Party of India (Maoist) (CPI-M). The combining of the two groups has created a fighting force with a cadre strength of 10,000–20,000. The ideology is based on Maoism, which the group regards as 'the higher stage of the Marxist-Leninist philosophy' (as quoted from its profile on the website South Asia Terrorism Portal). The CPI-M's goals are the abolition of class hierarchies and the establishment of a new democratic state under the leadership of the proletariat, based on socialist and communist ideas. The group is dedicated to using extreme violence in order to realize its aims, and is committed to the Maoist strategy of protracted armed struggle.

Members of the CPI-M have been responsible for the killing of numerous police officers, government officials, and teachers and other civilians. In 2009 the Indian government banned the CPI-M and what it sees as front organizations created by the group (see p. 103) in order to conceal its activities or provide it with logistical or financial support.

June	2005	Attack (with land mines, firearms and bows and arrows) on a village meeting called to discuss the boycott of the CPI-M, killing 8 people and injuring some 100
February	2006	Bombing of a truck carrying villagers returning from an anti-Maoist rally, killing at least 55 people and injuring more than 20
June	2010	Ambush of a security patrol and 3-hour gun battle, killing 26 people and injuring 7

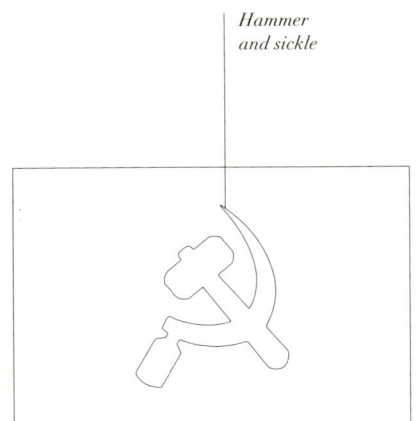

Hammer
and sickle

Five-pointed star

Independence
Democracy
Socialism

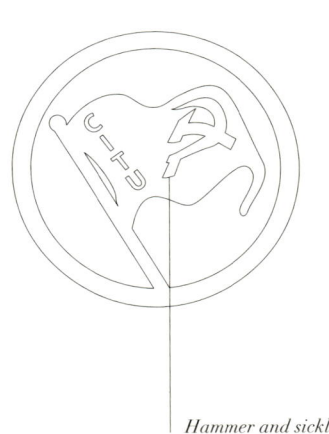

Hammer and sickle

Five-pointed star

Raised fists

COLOUR	PANTONE CODE	CMYK	RGB
	032	0.90.86.0	29.29.27
	072	100.88.0.5	36.53.136

Logo of the CPI-M

CPI-M front organization: Student Federation of India

CPI-M front organization:
Centre of Indian Trade Unions

CPI-M front organization:
Bank Employees Federation of India

The logos of the CPI-M and its front organizations share many elements. Recurring features are the use of the colour red, symbolizing socialist and communist ideology and revolution; the hammer and sickle, representing the worker; and the five-pointed star. This last feature can have several meanings, all of them in line with communist ideology. It can represent the five fingers of the worker's hand, the five continents (symbolizing global social revolution) and the five entities of a socialist society (workers, farmers, intellectuals, soldiers and youth). The two clenched fists in the BEFI logo represent unity and resistance.

18. COMMUNIST PARTY OF THE PHILIPPINES (CPP) / NEW PEOPLE'S ARMY (NPA)

Names in Filipino:
CPP: Partido Komunista ng Pilipinas / NPA: Bagong Hukbong Bayan

The Communist Party of the Philippines (CPP) was founded in 1968 and has operated clandestinely since its formation. Among its objectives are the overthrow of the Filipino government by means of an armed proletarian revolution, and its replacement with a new government based on communist principles. The CPP's ideology is based on Marxism, Leninism and Maoism.

The CPP's military wing, the New People's Army (NPA), was established in 1969 and until the mid-1970s was sponsored by China. The NPA's current cadre strength is approximately 16,000. It targets foreign investors and foreign-owned companies through kidnappings and extortion to fund its operations, and conducts assassinations of Filipino politicians, journalists and security officials.

September	1983	Killing of 39 soldiers of the Philippine Army and wounding of 17 others
October	2010	Attack on a convoy carrying election results in the Philippines, killing 6 people and injuring 12
April	2012	Ambush of a military convoy of the Philippine Army, killing 11 soldiers

Three armed people (two men, one woman)

Triangle containing five-pointed star

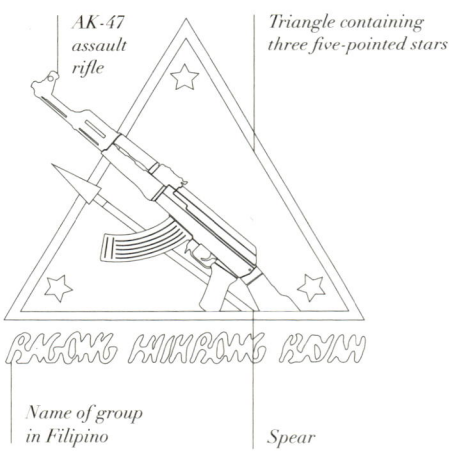

AK-47 assault rifle

Triangle containing three five-pointed stars

Name of group in Filipino

Spear

COLOUR	PANTONE CODE	CMYK	RGB
	1797	0.100.99.4	220.8.20
	116	0.16.100.0	255.211.0
	process black	0.0.0.100	29.29.27

Logo of the NPA

Variation of the NPA logo

The CPP uses no logo, but its military wing, the NPA, uses two. The one used most frequently, a black-and-white image, has as its central element a group of three people – one of them a woman, differentiated by her dress – each holding an AK-47 assault rifle. This symbolizes armed struggle by all members of the population and reflects socialist ideals, according to which everybody should be treated equally.

The NPA's other logo is a red triangle with a golden five-pointed star in each corner. It further shows an AK-47 assault rifle and a spear. The weapons symbolize the group's militancy; the spear links the struggle against oppression to pre-modern times.

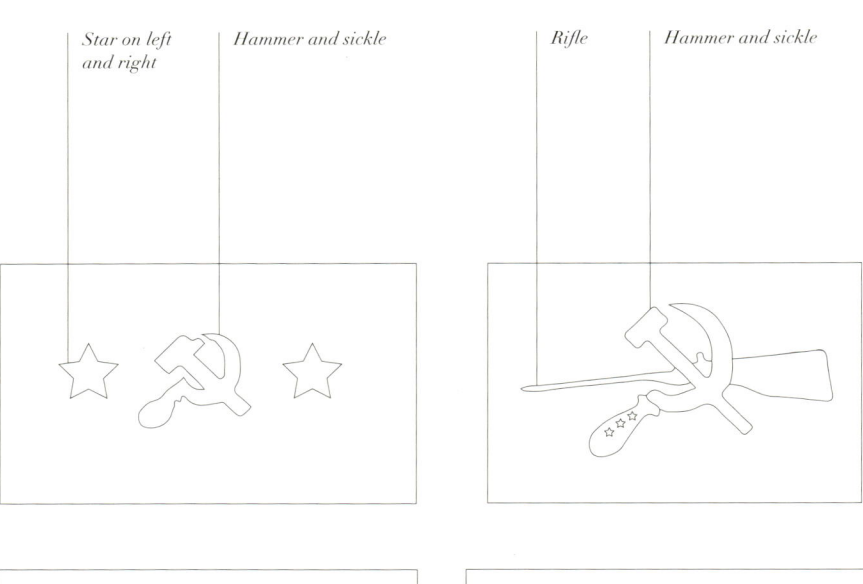

Star on left
and right

Hammer and sickle

Rifle

Hammer and sickle

Hammer and sickle

Variation of the NPA
logo (see p. 107)

COLOUR	PANTONE CODE	CMYK	RGB
	032	0.90.86.0	221.5.43
	116	0.16.100.0	255.211.0
	reflex blue	100.73.0.2	0.74.153
	process black	0.0.0.100	0.0.0

Flag of the CPP, 1968–86

Flag of the CPP, 1986–99

Flag of the CPP, 1999–present

Flag of the NPA

The CPP has used three different flags in its history, each showing variations of the hammer and sickle and five-pointed star symbols, representing socialist and communist ideals (see p. 103). The flag used from 1986 to 1999 also featured a rifle, representing the armed struggle the organization is prepared to employ in order to achieve its goals. All the CPP's flags, as well as that of the NPA, have a red background, symbolizing revolution; the gold elements symbolize justice, power and perfection. The NPA flag is based on one of its logos (see p. 107).

Communist Party of the Philippines (CPP) / New People's Army (NPA)

19. FEDERAZIONE ANARCHICA INFORMALE (FAI)

The Federazione Anarchica Informale ('informal anarchist federation'; FAI) is an umbrella insurrectionary anarchist organization established in Italy in 2003. The FAI is composed of various Italian groups that are united in their belief in revolutionary armed action, including the July 20th Brigade; the Five Cs; International Solidarity; and the Cooperative of Hand-Made Fire and Related Items. The groups act independently, but also under the banner of the FAI.

The FAI has stated that it targets 'the apparatus of control that is repressive and leading the democratic show that is the new European order' (as quoted by the BBC in 2003). It is opposed to the European Union (EU) and to Marxism, which it perceives to be just another type of oppressive authority. The current strength of the organization is not known. The FAI engages in bombings, and sends out threatening letters and propaganda to EU-related government offices in Italy, Germany and The Netherlands.

December	2003	Two bombs planted in bins outside the house of the European Commission president, Romano Prodi, in Bologna, Italy. No one is injured
June	2006	Bomb attack against the police school Fossano, Italy. No one is injured
March	2010	Menacing letter containing a bullet and the threat 'you will end up like a rat' sent to the Italian prime minister, Silvio Berlusconi

Two SC70/90 assault rifles
forming the letter 'A'

Flames   Name of group in Italian

Five-pointed star
containing the letter 'A'

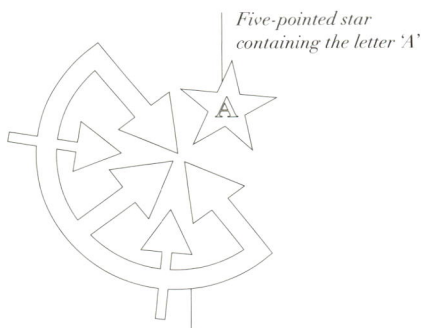

NUCLEO OLGA
FEDERAZIONE ANARCHICA INFORMALE
FRONTE RIVOLUZIONARIO INTERNAZIONALE

Five arrows linked
by a semicircle

Name of group and other related
organizations

COLOUR	PANTONE CODE	CMYK	RGB
▮	1797	0.100.99.4	220.8.20
▮	process black	0.0.0.100	0.0.0

Logo of the FAI

*Logo shared by FAI and
other anarchist groups*

**NUCLEO OLGA
FEDERAZIONE ANARCHICA INFORMALE
FRONTE RIVOLUZIONARIO INTERNAZIONAL**

The FAI logo features two Italian-army Beretta SC70/90 assault rifles, standing for the group's Italian origins. Red, which is associated with revolution, war, bloodshed and victory, signifies that the group engages in revolutionary armed action and believes it will eventually be victorious. Flames reinforce the group's commitment to violent means in order to achieve its goal of anarchy, the symbol for which is the letter 'A', formed by the two rifles. The letter is also seen in the logo the FAI shares with other groups related to it, in the five-pointed star symbolizing unity of all nations. The arrows pointing towards the same spot stand for the FAI's composition of various groups, called a <u>nucleo</u>, and their collective effort to replace the Italian governmental structure with anarchy.

20. GAMA'A AL-ISLAMIYYA (IG)

Name in Arabic: الجماعة الإسلامية

Transliteration: al-jema'ah al-islamiyah

Gama'a al-Islamiyya (Arabic for 'the Islamic group'; IG) was created as an umbrella organization for Egyptian militant student groups in the early 1970s, after the leadership of the »Muslim Brotherhood officially renounced violence. The organization advocated the overthrow of the secular Egyptian government and its replacement with an Islamic government. In the 1990s the IG committed armed attacks on officials of the Egyptian security forces and government, Egyptian Coptic Christians and foreign tourists.

The IG agreed a ceasefire with the Egyptian government in 1999. In 2006 »al-Qaeda's number two, Ayman al-Zawahiri, announced that the IG had merged with al-Qaeda, although the IG's leadership rejected this claim. With most of its members imprisoned (most notably the organization's spiritual leader, the cleric Omar Abdel-Rahman, who is serving a life sentence in the United States for his involvement in the truck bombing of the World Trade Center in New York in 1993), the group has not launched any attack since 1998. Following the revolution in 2011 that led to the resignation of the Egyptian president, Hosni Mubarak, the IG formed a political party, the Building and Development Party, which gained 13 seats in the 2011-12 elections.

June	1995	Assassination attempt against the Egyptian president, Hosni Mubarak, in Addis Ababa, Ethiopia, killing 2 people and injuring 1
September	1997	Ambush of a foreign tour bus near the Egyptian Museum in Cairo with firearms and petrol bombs, killing 10 people
November	1997	Militants shoot and knife to death 62 people, including 58 foreign tourists, at the Temple of Hatshepsut in Luxor, Egypt

Crossed swords

In Arabic, from the Qur'an (56:77):
'Truly, the Qur'an is noble'

Crescent moon

Name of group in Arabic

In Arabic, from the Qur'an
(8:60): 'Be prepared!'

COLOUR	PANTONE CODE	CMYK	RGB
	5535	66.0.57.82	17.60.43

The IG logo is similar to that of the »Muslim Brotherhood (MB),
but is in green rather than brown and features a crescent moon, c
symbol of Islamic identity. The colour green was used by the Prophet
Muhammad's tribe on flags. Muhammad was a fighter and a political
figure as well as a religious leader; thus, colouring the crescent
moon and the other elements of the logo green is a reference to a
militant and funcamentalist interpretation of Islam. By referencing
the elements and design of the MB logo, the IG acknowledges that its
spiritual roots lie in the MB, but by its use of the colour green it
communicates its political activism and militancy more aggressively.

21. GREAT EASTERN ISLAMIC RAIDERS FRONT (IBDA-C)

Name in Turkish: Islami Büyükdoğu Akıncılar Cephesi

The Great Eastern Islamic Raiders Front, also known by its Turkish-language initials I3DA-C, is a group of radical Sunni Salafis founded in 1985 as a breakaway faction of the Turkish Islamist political party the National Salvation Party. The IBDA-C follows the absolutist Büyük Doğu ('Great East') ideology, and promises to bring Muslims closer to success and salvation through the practice of Islam. The group perceives the Turkish secular regime as 'illegal', criticizes its cooperation with Western governments, and aims to destroy the Turkish secular state and constitutional system in order to establish an Islamic government based on sharia law, first in Turkey and then throughout the world.

The IBDA-C is most active in the Istanbul region, engaging in bombings, the throwing of Molotov cocktails, sabotage and assassinations, and attacks on civilian targets, such as bars, discotheques, charities and non-Muslim places of worship. It produces propagandist literature in which it announces its targets and invites members to launch independent attacks, and distributes it in bookshops and on the internet. The exact number of supporters is unknown but thought to be small. The IBDA-C has claimed responsibility for attacks that analysts believe are beyond its capabilities.

July	1993	Firebomb attack on a hotel in Sivas, Turkey, killing 37 people
November	2003	Truck suicide bombings of two synagogues in Istanbul, killing at least 24 people and injuring more than 255
November	2003	Truck suicide bombings of the Turkish headquarters of HSBC bank and the British consulate in Istanbul, killing 30 people and injuring 400; analysts suspect that »al-Qaeda is also responsible

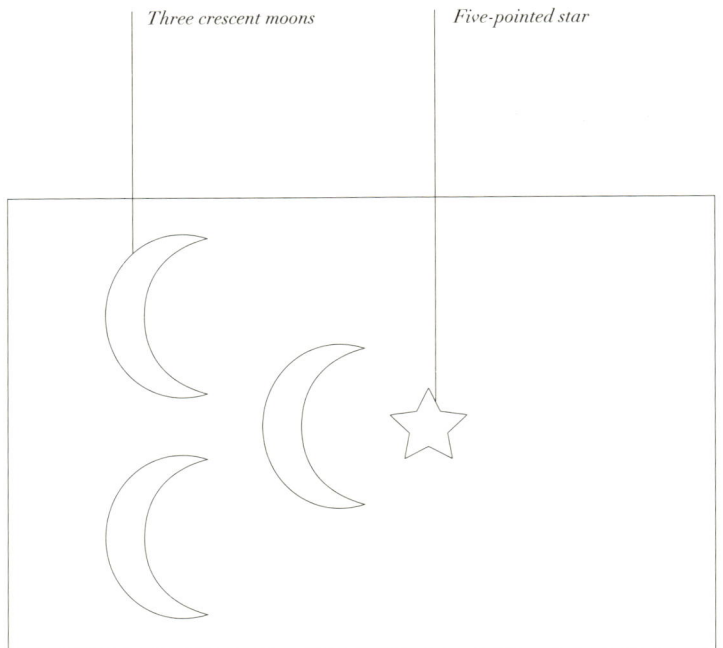

Three crescent moons   _Five-pointed star_

COLOUR	PANTONE CODE	CMYK	RGB
	293	100.57.0.2	0.95.170

The white crescent moon is a symbol of Islamic identity, evoking notions of purity and religious piety. The IBDA-C positions itself as the inheritor of the legacy of the Ottoman Caliphate, the empire established by Turkish tribes in north-western Anatolia (modern-day Turkey) in the late thirteenth century, and aims to re-establish the caliphate. The three crescent moons are a direct reference to the flag of the Ottoman Caliphate used between 1844 and 1923. The Ottoman Caliphate was the first government to feature the five-pointed star on its flag. Arguably, the star represents the Five Pillars of Islam, the five obligations that every Muslim must satisfy in order to live a good and responsible life. In Islam the colour blue is associated with Heaven. It is also the sacred colour of the whole Turkestan region, and a code for an easterly direction. Its use therefore suggests a reference to the planned expansion of the caliphate towards the east.

22. GRUPOS DE RESISTENCIA ANTIFASCISTA PRIMERO DE OCTUBRE (GRAPO)

The 'Antifascist Resistance Groups First of October' (GRAPO in its Spanish-language acronym) was founded in 1975 as the military wing of the Reconstituted Communist Party of Spain (abbreviated in Spanish as PCE-r), a banned political organization. The date in GRAPO's name refers to the killing of four Spanish policemen on 1 October 1975, the first violent action of the PCE-r.

The aim of GRAPO is to overthrow the Spanish government and replace it with a Marxist-Leninist government based on communist ideals. It has approximately twenty members. To oppose American military presence on Spanish territory and Spain's membership of NATO, the group has engaged in terrorist activities against the Spanish government and American military and industrial establishments. Types of attack have included killings, bombings, kidnappings and extortion from both individuals and businesses. In addition, to fund its operations the group has carried out numerous robberies. No successful terrorist action has been executed by GRAPO since 2002; however, in 2001, following the terrorist attacks against the World Trade Center in New York, the group publicly supported these attacks in a statement approving the destruction of the 'symbols of imperialist power'.

August	1975	Killing of 2 members of the Spanish Civil Guard in Madrid
June	1995	Kidnapping of the businessman Publio Cordon. His family pays a ransom of 400 million pesetas (€2.5 million), but he is not released. He is now known to have died in an escape attempt a few weeks after his abduction
May	2000	Murder of 2 security officers during an unsuccessful attempt to raid an armed truck carrying $2 million

Five-pointed star

Letters 'G' and 'R' combined
(for 'Grupos de Resistencia')

Submachine gun

Submachine gun

Abbreviation of the group's name in
German (Rote Armee Faktion)

Five-pointed star

COLOUR	PANTONE CODE	CMYK	RGB
	032	0.90.86.0	29.29.27
	151	0.48.95.0	244.151.18
	proces black	0.0.0.100	0.0.0

Logo of GRAPO

Logo of the German Rote Armee
Faktion (RAF), the inspiration
for the GRAPO logo

The GRAPO logo features a red five-pointed star, emphasizing the
group's ideological roots in communism. In communist imagery, the red
star symbolizes unity of all elements of a socialist society (workers,
farmers, intellectuals, soldiers and youth), as well as of all five
continents. The firearm (based on a combination of the German MP40
and the British Sterling L2A3 (Mark 4) submachine guns) stands for
the violent means GRAPO intends to use in order to achieve its aims.

The group's logo was inspired by that of the German left-wing guerrilla
group Rote Armee Faktion (RAF; also once known as the Baader-Meinhof
Gang), with which GRAPO shared a similar ideology. Most analysts
believe that the RAF was dissolved in 1998.

*Modified flag of the Second Spanish Republic,
adding a five-pointed star within a frame*

COLOUR	PANTONE CODE	CMYK	RGB
	185	0.91.76.0	214.23.42
	116	0.16.100.0	254.201.0
	252	24.56.0.0	181.113.168

The GRAPO flag is a modified version of the flag of the Second Spanish Republic (1931-39). The three colours represent the territories of the former Crown of Aragon and the regions of Castile and León, and thus symbolize a new era for Spain in which no part of the country would be excluded The GRAPO variant contains a red five-pointed star that stands for the Marxist-Leninist ideological foundation of the group (see p. 125). Using the flag of the Second Spanish Republic as a base evokes a historical connection between the objectives of early Spanish republicans and GRAPO's current aim of abolishing the Spanish monarchy.

23. HAMAS

Name in Arabic: حركة المقاومة الإسلامية / حمـاس
Transliteration (full name): harakat al-muqawamah al-islamiyyah

Hamas is a Palestinian Sunni Islamist movement aiming to establish an Islamic state based on sharia law in Palestine. In Arabic, the name 'Hamas' is both the acronym for 'Islamic resistance movement' and a word meaning '[religious] enthusiasm'.

Members of the Palestinian branch of the »Muslim Brotherhood founded Hamas in 1987, at the beginning of the six-year-long Palestinian uprising against the Israeli occupation of the Palestinian territories (a period known as the First Intifada), with Sheikh Ahmed Yassin as its spiritual leader. Hamas positions itself as the counterweight to the secular movement Fatah, co-founded in 1959 by Yasser Arafat, and has violently opposed any political compromise with Israel. It engages in armed assaults, assassinations, suicide bombings, hostage-taking and hijackings.

Hamas has a political wing responsible for ideological support and propaganda activities. As part of its ideology and to increase popular support, the group maintains an active network of social services within the Palestinian territories. In a decisive political victory in the Palestinian parliamentary elections of 2006, Hamas won 76 of the 132 seats (at the time of going to press, a date for new elections had yet to be confirmed).

February	1996	Bomb attacks on buses in Jerusalem, killing 28 people and injuring 80
March	2002	Suicide bombing at a hotel in Netanya, Israel, killing 30 people and injuring 140
August	2003	Suicide bombing of a bus in an ultra-Orthodox Jewish neighbourhood of Jerusalem, killing 18 people and injuring 100

Outline of Palestine

Dome of the Rock mosque, Jerusalem

Two Palestinian flags encircling the mosque,
each featuring one half of the shahada
('There is no god but God [Allah], and
Muhammad is His messenger')

In Arabic, full name of group:
Islamic Resistance Movement

Crossed swords, and beneath
them the word 'Palestine' in Arabic

COLOUR	PANTONE CODE	CMYK	RGB
	186	0.100.81.4	221.5.43
	356	95.0.100.27	0.125.50
	116	0.16.100.0	255.211.0
	reflex blue	100.73.0.2	0.74.153
	cool grey 9	1.0.0.51	156.156.158
	1817	0.90.100.66	109.27.0
	process black	0.0.0.100	29.29.27

The Dome of the Rock mosque in Jerusalem is the third holiest site in Islam. The Hamas logo uses it as a Palestinian national symbol. This is further reinforced by the Palestinian flag on either side of the mosque. Above it, the outline of Palestine is an indication that Hamas aims to reclaim the entire region, including Israel. Colouring the map green denotes that the land of Palestine belongs to Islam (see p. 117). The two crossed swords stand for the violent means that will safeguard the Palestinian nation; these pre-modern weapons further evoke notions of nobility and purity associated with the first generation of Muslims.

The shahada: 'There is no god but God [Allah],
and Muhammad is His messenger'

COLOUR	PANTONE CODE	CMYK	RGB
	356	95.0.100.27	0.125.50

Article Six of the Hamas charter states that the group 'strives to raise the banner of Allah over every inch of Palestine', while the Hamas flag features the shahada, the Muslim declaration of faith. Compared with other designs of the shahada, the distinctive element here is that the word 'Allah' protrudes above the rest of the text. This is done to reinforce the message that Allah (God) stands above everything else. The flag is green, a colour that is linked to the Prophet Muhammad (see p. 117). Colouring the flag green is an overtly political statement and shows that Hamas is not a secular or multi-confessional movement but a purely Islamic organization. Furthermore, it indicates that the state Hamas plans to establish will be based on sharia law.

24. HARAKAT AL-SHABAAB AL-MUJAHIDEEN (AL-SHABAAB)

Name in Arabic: حركة الشباب المجاهدين

Initially a loose network of Islamist groups opposed to the Ethiopian invasion of Somalia in 2006, Harakat al-Shabaab al-Mujahideen (Arabic for 'mujahideen youth movement'; commonly referred to simply as al-Shabaab) has evolved into a hierarchically organized Islamist extremist group. Al-Shabaab, which is ideologically motivated by the strict Salafi interpretation of Islam, endorses waging jihad against the international 'crusaders' and for the 'liberation' of the 'three holy sanctuaries', Mecca, Medina (both in modern-day Saudi Arabia) and Jerusalem, in Israel.

Al-Shabaab's decision-making structure is centralized. Non-Somali jihadists take exclusive tactical and operational command; loyal commanders selected from local clans administer al-Shabaab-controlled areas of Somalia. Funding comes from Saudi sources, both official (government, non-governmental organizations and foundations) and unofficial (private individuals and criminal groups). Other sources financing fighters' salaries (Singapore's International Centre for Political Violence and Terrorism Research estimates that fighters are paid $100-$300 a month) include networks of Somali exiles, fees charged to local merchants and businessmen, taxes collected at controlled ports and the sale of siezed goods, such as clothing and shoes.

March	2010	Multiple attacks against Somalia's Transitional Federal Government and the African Union Mission in Somalia, killing at least 60 people and wounding 160
August	2010	Suicide attacks in the Muna Hotel in Mogadishu, Somalia, killing 33 people, including 10 government officials
July	2011	Suicide bombings in Kampala, Uganda, killing some 80 people

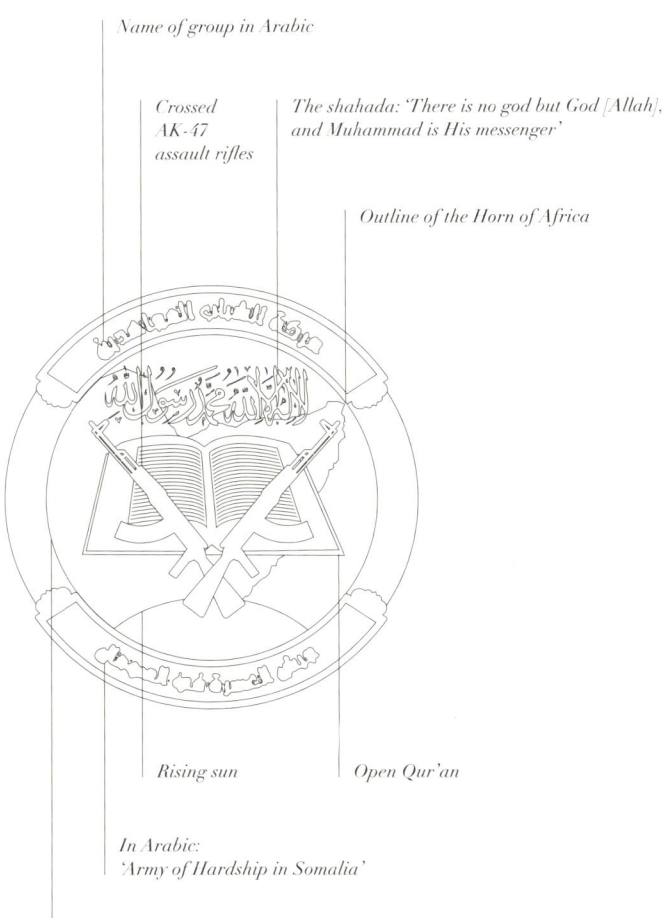

Name of group in Arabic

Crossed
AK-47
assault rifles

The shahada: 'There is no god but God [Allah],
and Muhammad is His messenger'

Outline of the Horn of Africa

Rising sun

Open Qur'an

In Arabic:
'Army of Hardship in Somalia'

Globe

COLOUR	PANTONE CODE	CMYK	RGB
	356	95.0.100.27	0.125.50
	1797	0.100.99.4	220.8.20
	process yellow	0.0.100.0	255.237.0
	175	0.65.100.70	125.62.0
	process black	0.0.0.100	0.0.0

The green globe represents al-Shabaab's global aspirations, while the outline of the Horn of Africa shows the group's primary geographical location. The open Qur'an highlights both the goal of establishing an Islamic state in Somalia and the centrality of Islam to the group's ideology. The shahada (the Muslim declaration of faith) immediately above the Qur'an further underlines the group's devotion and commitment to Islam; above this is the group's name. The crossed assault rifles symbolize violent struggle and suggest al-Shabaab's participation in the jihad movement. The text at the bottom translates as 'Army of Hardship in Somalia', and is a reference to the Army of Hardship that won the Battle of Badr against 'disbelievers' in Mecca during the time of the Prophet Muhammad (see p. 43). Above this rises the sun, symbolizing a new beginning.

First part of the shahada:
'There is no god but God [Allah]'

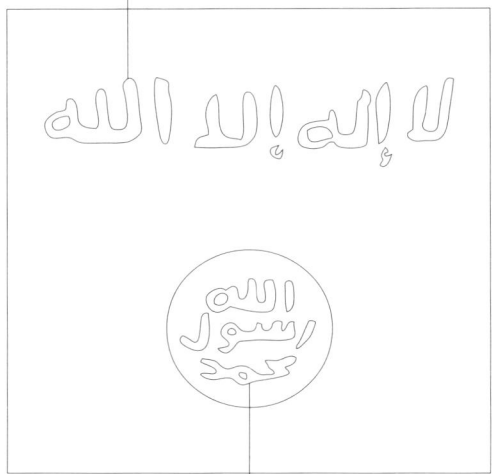

Second part of the shahada:
'Muhammad is His messenger'

COLOUR	PANTONE CODE	CMYK	RGB
■	process black	0.0.0.100	0.0.0

Al-Shabaab uses two flags, both of which feature the shahada, the Muslim declaration of faith. The first flag (shown above), referred to as <u>al-raya</u>, is based on the black battle flag of the Prophet Muhammad (see p. 51), and is similar to the one used by the group »al-Qaeda in Iraq. The second flag, al-Shabaab's administration flag, is the same as the first but with the colours reversed; it is the most likely of the two to become the official flag of the Islamic caliphate that al-Shabaab hopes to establish.

25. HARAKAT UL-MUJAHIDEEN (HUM)

Name in Urdu: حرکت المجابدین

Harakat ul-Mujahideen (Urdu for 'movement of the mujahideen'; HUM), formerly known as Harakat al-Ansar ('movement of the supporters'; HAA), is a separatist militant Islamic group based in Pakistan and operating primarily in Kashmir. Its main goal is independence for Indian-administered Kashmir. As HAA, the group was established in 1980, mainly to send volunteers to Afghanistan to assist rebels fighting the Soviet invasion. HUM is politically aligned with the Pakistani radical party Jamiat-e Ulema-e-Islam, Fazlur Rehman faction (JUI-F). Fazlur Rehman Khalil was a long-time leader of HUM, until he stepped down in 2000 – according to open sources, owing to pressure by the Pakistani government. He was one of the signatories to the fatwa issued by »al-Qaeda founder Osama bin Laden in 1998, calling for attacks on American and Western interests.

The current leader of HUM is Farooq Kashmiri, a former military commander from Kashmir. The group undertakes armed assaults, kidnappings and hijackings. Coalition forces involved in the NATO-led invasion of Afghanistan allege that HUM operated terrorist training camps in eastern Afghanistan, until these were destroyed by Coalition airstrikes in 2001.

December	1999	Hijacking of an India Airlines aeroplane, resulting in the release of Masood Azhar, an HAA leader and the founder of »Army of Muhammad
March	2003	Firearm attack on a police post in the Udhampur district of the Indian state of Jammu and Kashmir, killing 11 people and injuring 9
February	2009	Death threat against the leader of the Indian Bharatiya Janata Party, Lalchand Kishen Advani

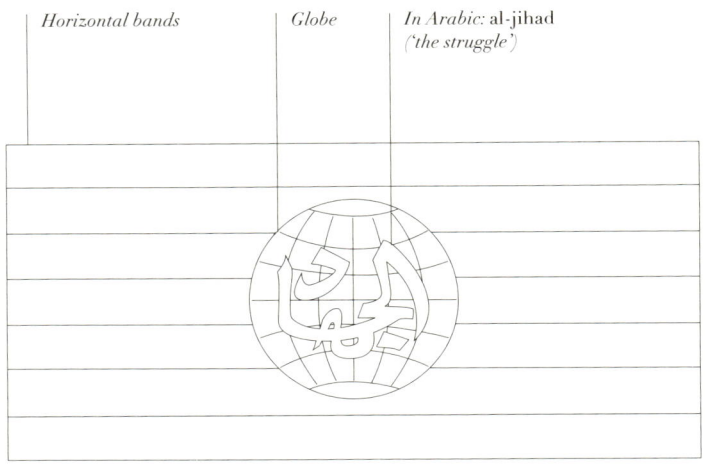

Horizontal bands   Globe   *In Arabic:* al-jihad
                                         (*'the struggle'*)

COLOUR	PANTONE CODE	CMYK	RGB
	356	95.0.100.27	0.125.50
	110	0.12.100.7	244.207.0
	process black	0.0.0.100	0.0.0

The HUM flag features at its centre a globe with the word 'al-jihad' written inside it, symbolizing the group's global jihadist objectives. The arrangement of the stripes is taken directly from the flag of Harakat al-Ansar, the group's predecessor. The black stripes are linked to the black battle flag of the Prophet Muhammad (see p. 51), evoking a historical sense of the concept of jihad. The colour green refers to the Prophet Muhammad personally (see p. 117). White symbolizes purity, piety and religious authority.

26. HEZBOLLAH

Name in Arabic: حزب الله

In 1982, a group of Iranian clergymen founded a loose network of Shia militias in southern Lebanon to pursue Iranian objectives in the region, and in particular to carry out tasks in confrontation with Israel. These militias were trained by members of the Army of the Guardians of the Islamic Revolution (a branch of Iran's military; known as IRGC), which analysts allege still provides military and financial support to the network. The name 'Hezbollah' (Arabic for 'party of Allah') was officially adopted in 1985. The group has approximately 200,000 supporters, and is currently active in all Shia areas of Lebanon. Among the aims expressed in an open letter in 1985 were the foundation of a global Islamic state; the destruction of Israel; opposition to the United States; and the establishment of a Shia imamate. Hezbollah is among the most technically capable and heavily armed terrorist groups in the world.

Alongside its militia and terrorist activities, Hezbollah operates a network of social programmes and political operations. The group is governed by the Majlis al-Shura council, which consits of some 200 representatives from influential clans and is led by a secretary-general (currently Hassan Nasrallah). Hezbollah and its allies have dominated the Lebanese parliament since June 2011.

October	1983	Two suicide truck bombings on the US Marine barracks and the French military base in Beirut, Lebanon, killing 299 American and French military personnel
July	2006	Attack on an Israeli army patrol leads to the kidnapping of 2 soldiers and the killing of 3, starting a conflict with Israel that lasts for 34 days
May	2008	Two-week armed takeover of West Beirut, after the Lebanese government announces its plan to remove Hezbollah's telephone network

In Arabic, from the Qur'an (5:56):
'Then the party of Allah will be victorious'

Clenched fist holding a rifle

Seven-leafed branch

Globe

فإن حزب الله هم الغالبون

المقاومة الإسلامية في لبنان

Book representing the Qur'an

Name of group in Kufic script

In Arabic: 'Islamic Resistance Movement in Lebanon'

COLOUR	PANTONE CODE	CMYK	RGB
🟩	355	94.0.100.0	0.155.62
🟥	485	0.95.100.0	228.35.19

Hezbollah's logo is a variation of that of the IRGC (see p. 149). Above the logo is Hezbollah's slogan in Arabic, a verse from the Qur'an (5:56) that translates as 'Then the party of Allah will be victorious'. This represents the essence of Hezbollah's promise. Green is associated with the Prophet Muhammad (see p. 117) and red with Imam Hassan, a seventh-century martyr and the son of Muhammad's daughter Fatima. Beneath the globe is a visualization of the word 'Hezbollah' in Kufic script, the oldest form of the various Arabic scripts and the one used to write the first copies of the Qur'an. From this word, a clenched fist holding a rifle emerges from the letter known as 'alef', the first letter of the word 'Allah'.

Globe   Clenched fist holding a rifle

Branch with nine leaves

In Arabic, from the Qur'an (8:60):
'And make ready against them
all you can of power'

Name of group in Persian, and, to its
left, a book representing the Qur'an

In Persian numerals, the year the group was
founded: 1357 (Jalali or Persian calendar;
1978 in the Gregorian or Western calendar)

COLOUR	PANTONE CODE	CMYK	RGB
▮	reflex blue	100.89.0.0	8.41.148

This, the logo of the IRGC, a branch of the Iranian army, is the one
on which Hezbollah has based its own (see p. 147). The clenched fist
holding a rifle stands for armed resistance, while the wheat-like
plant represents growth and prosperity. The book beneath the arm is a
reference to the Qur'an and gives religious legitimacy to both groups
and their acts. In the background, the globe signifies the worldwide
ambitions of the Shia Islamic revolution that the groups represent.

27. HIZB-UT-TAHRIR (HUT)

Name in Arabic: حزب التحرير

Hizb-ut-Tahrir (Arabic for 'party of liberation'; HUT), an international Islamic political organization, was founded in 1953 in East Jerusalem, which at the time was controlled by Jordan. Both open and underground branches are maintained by HUT in several dozen countries around the world. It rejects nation states and aims to establish a single Islamic state, based on pure Islamic principles. Its ideology proclaims that the re-establishment of an Islamic caliphate begins in all Muslim countries, and that ultimately the caliphate will include the entire world.

In HUT ideology, offensive jihad is legitimate only as a means to achieve the foreign policy objectives of the Islamic state; therefore, it is allowable to kill apostates only if an Islamic state exists. The group's political goal is the destruction of Israel and its inhabitants. There is no evidence that HUT has military capabilities, and as a group it has never been involved in terrorism. However, some analysts perceive HUT to be an intellectual forerunner of violence and suggest that it has radicalized people who might at some later time channel their activism into terrorist activities.

	1978	HUT states that Muslims have reached a state of total surrender to other religions, and need to rise again
	1998	HUT states that an Islamic caliphate is now the desire of all Muslims
July	2009	HUT holds a conference entitled 'Fall of Capitalism and Rise of Islam' in Illinois, its first major event in the United States

Black battle flag featuring the shahada: 'There is no god but God [Allah], and Muhammad is His messenger'

Globe

HIZB-UT-TAHRIR

تأسس سنة ١٣٧٢ ٥ ١٩٥٣م

In Arabic: 'Founded in the year 1372 [Hijri or Islamic calendar] – 1953 [Gregorian or Western calendar]'

Name of group in Arabic

COLOUR	PANTONE CODE	CMYK	RGB
	186	0.100.81.4	221.5.43
	process black	0.0.0.100	0.0.0

HIZB-UT-TAHRIR

The globe in HUT's logo represents the group's worldwide reach as well as its global ambitions as advocated through its ideology. The objective of establishing an Islamic caliphate is symbolized by the black al-raya flag featuring the shahada, the Muslim declaration of faith. The Prophet Muhammad was the first to use the al-raya as a battle flag (see p. 51). In this sense the al-raya is associated with religious revolt and battle, and thus jihad. That it is shown rising above the globe suggests a global jihadi aim.

28. HIZBUL MUJAHIDEEN (HM)

Name in Arabic: حزب المجاهدين

The goal of Hizbul Mujahideen (Arabic for 'party of the mujahideen'; HM), the militant wing of Pakistan's largest Islamic political party, the Jamaat-e-Islami (JEI), is the 'liberation' of Indian-administered Kashmir and its accession to Pakistan, although reports on open sources suggest that some of its cadres support the total independence of Kashmir. These sources also suggest that HM was founded by JEI in 1989 at the behest of Pakistan's Inter-Services Intelligence, the largest of the country's three intelligence services. The group, currently led by Syed Salahuddin, is headquartered in Muzaffarabad in Pakistan and has more than 100 members, mostly based in the Indian state of Jammu and Kashmir; it was also reported to have trained and operated in Afghanistan until the »Taliban assumed power there in 1996.

The acts HM primarily engages in are bombings, armed assaults and assassinations against Indian government and law-enforcement representatives in Jammu and Kashmir. In 1997 the group began to operate in tandem with the Pakistan-based »Lashkar-e-Tayyiba.

May	2004	Bombing of a bus in the village of Woodsa in the Indian state of Jammu and Kashmir, killing 28 Indian security personnel
July	2005	Car bombing of a military convoy in Srinagar, Jammu and Kashmir, killing 8 people and injuring 16
June	2006	Kidnapping of 15 people from Kulgan, Jammu and Kashmir, in tandem with »Lashkar-e-Tayyiba, torturing and killing 10 people and injuring 4

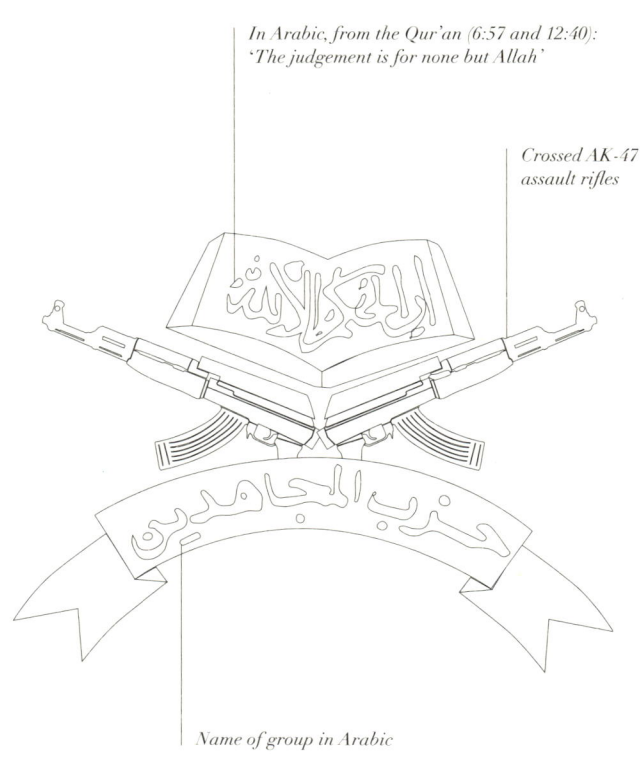

In Arabic, from the Qur'an (6:57 and 12:40):
'The judgement is for none but Allah'

Crossed AK-47
assault rifles

Name of group in Arabic

COLOUR	PANTONE CODE	CMYK	RGB
	348	100.0.85.24	0.126.72
	186	0.100.81.4	221.5.43
	429	3.0.0.32	175.180.183
	process black	0.0.0.100	29.29.27

At the centre of the HB logo are two AK-47 assault rifles, symbolizing the group's militancy and use of violent means to promote Islam and achieve Kashmiri secession from India. The Qur'an at the top stands for the group's ideological foundation in Islam. On its pages, a Qur'anic verse (6:57 and 12:40), which translates as 'The judgement is for none but Allah', confers religious legitimacy on the group's actions and denotes that it is following the path set out in the Qur'an. The colour green indicates that the ideology is not only religious but also political (see p. 117).

29. HOFSTADGROEP (HG)

Hofstadgroep (Dutch for 'group of the capital city'; HG) is the name used by the Dutch secret service, the AIVD, to refer to a Netherlands-based group of radical Muslims comprising mainly Dutch-Moroccans and reportedly one native Dutchman. The group is said to be guided by Redouan al-Issar, a Syrian who is by profession a geologist, and influenced by the Takfir wal-Hijra ideology, a school of thought that originated in Egypt and advocates the spread of Islam through immigration, and the annihalation of 'infidels' if they will not accept Islam.

Analysts consider the HG to be a self-generated autonomous Islamist terrorist network, and believe it has about twenty members. From 2002, the group interacted on the Microsoft Network and reportedly met regularly, either at the Salafist As-Soennah mosque in The Hague or at the home of the HG member Mohammed Bouyeri in Amsterdam, to discuss religious and political issues. The group ceased its activities when most of its members were arrested in 2004.

November	2004	HG member Mohammed Bouyeri shoots the Dutch film-maker and columnist Theo van Gogh 8 times, killing him on the spot, then tries to decapitate him and pins a 5-page letter to his chest with a knife

In Dutch and Arabic: 'Lions of Monotheism'

Sun

Qur'an featuring the shahada: 'There is no god but God [Allah], and Muhammad is His messenger'

Lions of the Dutch royal coat of arms, on right and left

In Dutch:
'Mujahideen of the Polder'

Crossed swords

COLOUR	PANTONE CODE	CMYK	RGB
	356	95.0.100.27	0.125.50
	1797	0.100.99.4	220.8.20
	012	0.4.100.0	255.231.0
	021	0.53.100.0	242.140.0
	process cyan	100.0.0.0	0.159.227
	175	0.65.100.70	125.62.0
	process black	0.0.0.100	0.0.0

The group is referred to as the Hofstadgroep by the Dutch authorities, but on its logo it announces itself as the Leeuwen van Tawheed ('Tawheed' being the Arabic for 'monotheism'). The logo combines Dutch and radical Islamist elements. On either side are two lions, as featured on the royal coat of arms of The Netherlands, representing the regional identity of the group. Regional identity is further reinforced by the orange colouring of the script; the green, flat background; and the word 'polder' (a low-lying area of land, which in The Netherlands is typically reclaimed land). The Qur'an in the centre shows the shahada, the Muslim declaration of faith. A representation of the sun is used to illuminate the Qur'an and give it a divine colouring. The two swords symbolize the violent reality of the jihadi struggle, and link jihad to early Islamic history.

30. HOLY LAND FOUNDATION FOR RELIEF AND DEVELOPMENT (HLF)

The Holy Land Foundation for Relief and Development (HLF) was established in 1989 as an Islamic charitable foundation with headquarters in Richardson, Texas, and became the largest such organization in the United States. It was part of a larger organization set up in North America by the »Muslim Brotherhood; on its website, its stated mission was to 'find and implement practical solutions for human suffering through humanitarian programs that impact the lives of the disadvantaged, disinherited and displaced peoples suffering from man-made and natural disasters'. Over the years the HLF raised more than $12 million in the United States, and transferred the monies to charitable organizations that operated in the Palestinian territories and were connected or controlled by »Hamas. Reports in open sources suggest that these funds were used to support schools that encouraged children to become suicide bombers, and to recruit suicide bombers by offering support to their families.

In 2008 five of the HLF s members and former fundraisers were convicted in the United States of providing material and logistical support to foreign terrorist organizations, as well as of tax fraud and money laundering, and were given sentences ranging from fifteen to sixty-five years in prison.

December	2001	The HLF is shut down by US authorites and its assets are frozen
July	2007	The first trial of the HLF for funding terrorist organizations is declared a mistrial becouse the jurors are deadlocked
August	2008	A retrial, dubbed the 'largest terrorism financing prosecution in American history', convicts the HLF on 108 charges, including money laundering and conspiracy to provide material support to a foreign terrorist organization

Two hands   Dome of a mosque

HOLY LAND FOUNDATION

Graphic element possibly
representing a window or a
niche in the wall of a mosque

Outline of Palestine

COLOUR	PANTONE CODE	CMYK	RGB
	113	0.7.66.0	255.231.111
	black 5	0.40.22.87	67.47.46

The charitable activities of the HLF are symbolized by the two helping hands supporting the base of a mosque dome and forming a protective frame around an outline of Palestine. The dome reinforces the organization's Islamic identity. The outline of Palestine stands for the main focus of the organization's charitable activities; the oval-topped element within it is possibly a mosque window, or a <u>mihrab</u>, a niche in the wall of a mosque that indicates the direction of Mecca and thus the direction in which Muslims should pray.

31. INDIAN MUJAHIDEEN (IM)

Name in Hindi: इंडियन मुजाहिदीन

Indian Mujahideen (IM) is a radical, militarized Sunni Muslim organization that emerged in about 2001 from within the banned Students Islamic Movement of India. Ideologically, IM follows the Deobandi school of Sunni Islam, which practises a rigid, puritanical version of Islam and advocates the use of jihad for Islamization. The organization rejects Hinduism (the majority religion in India), secularism, democracy and nationalism. It advocates waging jihad against non-Muslims, and the establishment of a government based on the Qur'an. Its stated goal is the 'liberation' of India from the influence of Western materialism, and its conversion into an Islamic society.

The organization became known to the public in 2007 when it claimed responsibility for serial bomb blasts in the Indian state of Uttar Pradesh that killed and wounded scores of people. It has predominantly conducted bombings with self-manufactured explosive devices, and has sent warning emails to the media prior to its attacks. Journalists report that IM has been receiving financial assistance from organizations based in Saudi Arabia and Kuwait.

July	2006	Suspected role in the bombing of a train and railway station in Mumbai, India, killing 209 people and injuring more than 700
May	2008	Series of 9 bombs in Jaipur, India, killing 60 people and injuring 200
September	2008	Series of 5 bombs in markets in New Delhi, India, killing 26 people and injuring some 100

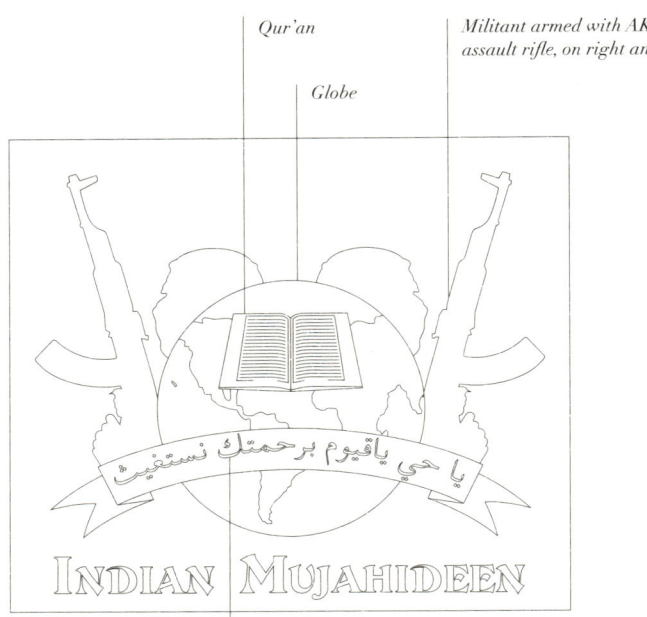

Qur'an

Globe

Militant armed with AK-47
assault rifle, on right and left

In Arabic: 'O Allah, the Ever Living,
the Sustainer of existence, we beg Your mercy'

COLOUR	PANTONE CODE	CMYK	RGB
	1235	0.29.91.0	252.189.27
	355	94.0.100.0	0.155.62
	1817	0.90.100.66	109.27.0
	2768	100.78.0.44	12.44.101
	311	63.0.12.0	82.193.221
	process black	0.0.0.100	29.29.27

The superimposition of the Qur'an over the globe represents IM's global Islamization efforts, and indicates that the group advocates an Islamic caliphate based on sharia law. The group's rejection of nationalism is illustrated by the lack of national borders on the globe. Two men holding AK-47 assault rifles symbolize IM's belief that Islamization requires violent and militant means. The text on the banner is a saying ascribed to the Prophet Muhammad (a hadith); it is taken from a sentence he is said to have used when a matter grieved him. It is an act of supplication, which is legitimate according to Sunni Islam's Deobandi school of thought, to which the group adheres.

32. ISLAMIC JIHAD MOVEMENT IN PALESTINE (IJMP)

Name in Arabic: حركة الجهاد الإسلامي في فلسطين

Transliteration: harakat al-jihad al-islami fi filastin

Sunni Palestinian students and members of the »Muslim Brotherhood founded the Islamic Jihad Movement in Palestine (also known as Palestinian Islamic Jihad; IJMP) in Egypt in the late 1970s. The founders, disillusioned with Muslim Brotherhood's non-violent position and its lack of commitment to the Palestinian cause, advocated violence as the only way to destroy Israel and establish an Islamic regime within that country's borders.

Although the IJMP is headquartered in Syria, its main support base is in the West Bank, the Gaza Strip and southern Lebanon. It has fewer than 1000 members. The group rejects any peace treaty with Israel and refuses to negotiate or engage in the diplomatic process. Unlike other Palestinian separatist groups, it does not participate in the political process, and it opposes the Palestinian Authority, the administrative body that governs the Gaza Strip and the West Bank. The military wing of the IJMP, the al-Quds Brigades, is responsible for terrorist attacks in the form of suicide bombings, shootings and the launching of rockets at Israeli targets. The IJMP is aligned with »Hezbollah, despite sectarian differences between the two groups, while a substantial part of its funding comes from Iran.

January	1995	Suicide bombing at the Beit Lid Junction, an important crossroads between Tel Aviv and Haifa in central Israel, killing 18 soldiers and 1 civilian
October	2003	Suicide bombing of a beachfront restaurant in Haifa, Israel, killing 21 people and injuring 60
April	2006	Suicide attack near a bus station in Tel Aviv, killing 11 people and injuring 68

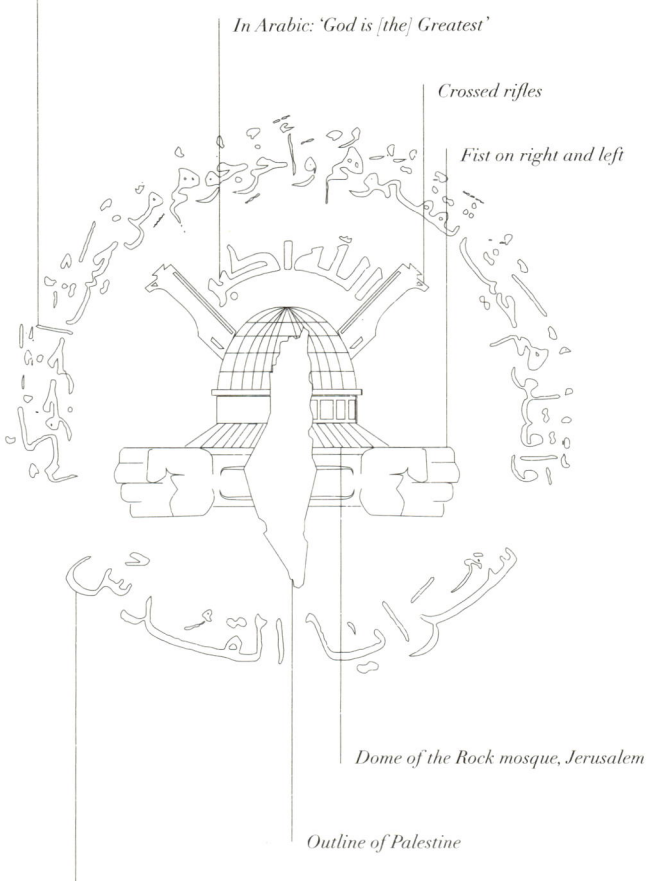

In Arabic, from the Qur'an (29:69): 'And for those who strive for Us, We will surely guide them to Our ways. And indeed, Allah is with the doers of good'

In Arabic: 'God is [the] Greatest'

Crossed rifles

Fist on right and left

Dome of the Rock mosque, Jerusalem

Outline of Palestine

Name of group in Arabic

COLOUR	PANTONE CODE	CMYK	RGB
	193	0.100.66.13	206.5.56
	364	65.0.100.42	69.124.31
	8580	31.50.75.28	150.110.64
	process black	0.0.0.100	0.0.0

The Dome of the Rock mosque in Jerusalem, shown in the centre of the
IJMP logo, is among the holiest sites in Islam. Owing to its location
in Palestine, it serves as a national symbol. Two rifles and two
fists form a protective frame for the mosque and thus the Palestinian
nation; these elements also refer to the group's militancy and its
commitment to jihad in order to liberate Palestine from perceived
Israeli occupation. The takbir (an Arabic phrase translated as 'God
is [the] Greatest') and the verse from the Qur'an highlight the group's
ideological roots in Islam. The colour red symbolizes both blood
and victory, and stresses that the current jihadi campaign will be
victorious. This is further emphasized and given religious legitimacy
by the Qur'anic verse. At the bottom, the group's name is in green,
which gives it added Islamic character (see p. 117).

33. ISLAMIC MOVEMENT OF UZBEKISTAN (IMU)
Name in Uzbek (Cyrillic script): Ўзбекистон Исломий Ҳаракати
Transliteration: oʻzbekiston islomiy harakati

The Islamic Movement of Uzbekistan (IMU) is a coalition of Islamist militants from Central Asian states, with recruits primarily including Uzbeks, Tajiks, Kyrgyz, Chechens and Uighurs. It was formed in 1991 with the aims of overthrowing Uzbekistan's secular regime and establishing in its place an Islamic state through the application of sharia law; however, it has been generally unable to operate in Uzbekistan. During the Tajik civil war (1992-97) the IMU's leader, Juma Namangani, established a base for his fighters in Tajikistan. The IMU relocated to Afghanistan in the late 1990s.

In 2001 the IMU expanded its territorial focus to encompass an area stretching from the Caucasus to China's western province of Xinjiang, under the new banners of the Islamic Party of Turkestan and the Islamic Movement of Turkestan. The group's fewer than 1000 militants fight alongside the »Taliban in Afghanistan. The IMU engages predominantly in bombings and assassinations, targeting government officials in Uzbekistan and Tajikistan; attacks against tourists are also common.

February	1999	Series of 5 car bombs in Tashkent, Uzbekistan, in an attempt to assassinate the president, Islam Karimov, killing 16 people and injuring more than 130
August	2010	Killing of 6 guards during a prison break in Dushanbe, Tajikistan, in which 25 IMU militants escape
September	2010	Ambush of Tajik troops in the Rasht Valley, Tajikistan, killing 25 soldiers and injuring 20

Globe with the Qur'an superimposed

*In Arabic, on the left-hand page, from the Qur'an (2:2):
'This is the Book about which there is no doubt, a guidance
for those who are conscious of Allah'
On the right-hand page: the letters alef (A), lam (L) and
mim (M), which open chapter 2 of the Qur'an. Only Allah
knows their precise meanings.*

Above the globe, in Arabic, the word 'Allah'

*The shahada: 'There is no
god but God [Allah], and
Muhammad is His messenger'*

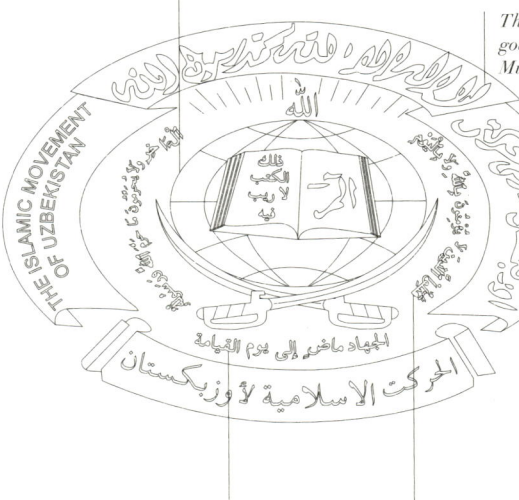

*In banner, on right and
at bottom of logo: name
of group in Arabic*

*To right and left of globe,
in Arabic, from the Qur'an
(9:29): 'Fight against those
who do not believe in Allah,
nor in the Last Day, nor
forbid that which has been
forbidden by Allah and
His messenger'*

*Crossed sabres; below them,
in Arabic: 'Jihad until the day
of Resurrection'*

COLOUR	PANTONE CODE	CMYK	RGB
	process yellow	0.0.100.0	255.240.0
	1797	0.100.100.0	224.0.27
	process black	0.0.0.100	255.255.255

The IMU logo makes numerous references to the Qur'an. This demonstrates the group's strong ideological commitment to Islam, which is further reinforced by the shahada, the Muslim declaration of faith. The IMU's aim of establishing an Islamic caliphate is illustrated by the super-imposition of the Qur'an over the globe and the word 'Allah' hovering above it. The other elements of the logo are shared with that of the IMU's successor, the Islamic Party of Turkestan (IPT; see p. 179).

Globe with the Qur'an superimposed;
above them, from the Qur'an (6:57
and 12:40): 'The judgement is for
none but Allah'

Middle ring, in Arabic:
At top, from the Qur'an (8:39): 'And
fight them until all opposition ends
and all submit to Allah'

At bottom, from the Qur'an (4:59): 'O
you who believe! Obey Allah and obey
the Messenger, and those in authority
among you'

Outer ring, in Arabic:
At bottom: 'Islamic Movement
of Turkestan'
On the right: name of group in Arabic:
Islamic Party of Turkestan
At top, the shahada: 'There is no god
but God [Allah], and Muhammad is
His messenger'

Crossed sabres

COLOUR	PANTONE CODE	CMYK	RGB
	process yellow	0.0.100.0	255.240.0
	1235	0.29.91.0	250.189.26
	2395	25.100.0.0	168.0.124
	process black	0.0.0.100	0.0.0

The logo of the IMU's successor, the Islamic Party of Turkestan (IPT), is based on that of the IMU (p. 177). The crossed sabres symbolize jihad. As a pre-modern weapon, the sword links the current jihadi struggle to early Islamic history, and portrays the current efforts as an extension of the early jihad campaigns.

34. IZZ AD-DIN AL-QASSAM BRIGADES (IDQ)

Name in Arabic: كتائب الشهيد عز الدين القسام

Transliteration: katacib al-shahid ezzedeen al-qassam

The Izz ad-Din al-Qassam Brigades (IDQ) is part of the Palestinian Sunni Islamist movement »Hamas. It was founded in 1992 as the armed element of Hamas's military wing, and is named after a Muslim leader in the fight against British, French and Zionist organizations in the Levant in the 1920s and 1930s. Often referred to as the 'Executive Force', IDQ is meant to provide a coordinated military response for Hamas. It operates independently from other sections of Hamas. It has conducted many guerrilla attacks and suicide bombings against Israeli civilian and military targets, as well as attacks against rivals in the Palestinian nationalist organization Fatah and Palestinians suspected of collaborating with Israel. Israeli sources estimate that the group has some 20,000 fighters.

Militant members of the brigade wear a black hood with a green headband. Those about to undertake a suicide operation are often seen posing in front of the green flag of Hamas before their mission.

June	2001	Suicide bombing at a nightclub in Tel Aviv, Israel, killing 21 people and injuring 120
March	2002	Suicide bombing at a hotel in Netanya, Israel, killing 30 people and injuring 140
June	2006	In tandem with »Army of Islam, kidnapping of the Israeli soldier Gilad Shalit, who remains in captivity for 5 years until released in exchange for 1027 Hamas and other Palestinian prisoners

Dome of the Rock
mosque, Jerusalem

In Arabic, from the Qur'an (8:17):
'You did not kill them, but it was
Allah [God] who killed them'

Name of group in Arabic

Person in keffiyeh (see pp. 266–67)
with headband bearing the shahada;
M16 assault rifle in his right hand,
the Qur'an in his left

Green flag featuring the shahada:
'There is no god but God [Allah],
and Muhammad is His messenger'

COLOUR	PANTONE CODE	CMYK	RGB
	7503	0.12.35.25	207.187.151
	600	0.0.29.0	255.249.202
	116	0.16.100.0	255.211.0
	485	0.95.100.0	228.35.19
	355	94.0.100.0	0.155.62
	process black	0.0.0.100	0.0.0

The IDQ is one of several Palestinian groups to feature the Dome of the Rock mosque, the third most holy site in Islam, on its logo. The mosque's location in Jerusalem, which is located in modern-day Israel but would become the capital of the Palestinian state the groups are fighting for, also makes it a symbol of Palestinian nationalism and an expression of the idea that Jerusalem and the whole of Palestine should belong to Muslims. Because of the mosque's religious and pan-Islamic connotations, its graphic representation serves as an inspirational symbol of jihad and martyrdom for the Palestinian nation. It confers religious legitimacy to militant activism and evokes a sense of national duty. Militancy, further symbolized by the firearm, is also given legitimacy by the verse from the Qur'an that runs along the top of the logo. The colour green gives the logo added Islamic character (see p. 117).

35. JEMMAH ANSHORUT TAUHID (JAT)

Name in Arabic: جماعة أنصار التوحيد

Transliteration: jamma ansar ut-tauhid

Jemmah Anshorut Tauhid (Arabic for 'group of the supporters of monotheism'; JAT), founded in 2008 in Indonesia, is a non-governmental organization facilitating public outreach and the teaching of Islam. It is currently led by the Indonesian radical cleric Abu Bakar Ba'asyir. The banner raised at JAT's formal inauguration proclaimed that the group aimed to 'revitalize the Islamic movement in support of full victory for the struggle of the Indonesian faithful'.

The organization is rooted in puritanical Salafi ideology, with an emphasis on jihad. It advocates the establishment of an Islamic caliphate and the full implementation of sharia law, and its teachings highlight defensive jihad against Islam's enemies. According to these teachings, jihad can be waged through 'dissemination of knowledge, physical battle, donation of property and by the pen' (as quoted from the International Crisis Group; see p. 330). The organization asserts that it operates within the law. It has not claimed responsibility for a terrorist attack, but is suspected by the Indonesian government of being involved in radicalizing its members and facilitating attacks.

November	2008	JAT publicly defends the militant Ali Ghufron (also known as Mukhlas), convicted of leading the Bali bombings of 2002, at the time of his execution
May	2010	Three senior JAT members are charged with raising funds for a training camp in the province of Aceh, Indonesia
September	2011	Suicide bombing of a church in Solo, on the Indonesian island of Java, killing 2 people and injuring 22

In Arabic, the words 'Sunna' (left-hand page) and 'Qur'an' (right-hand page)

A variation of the shahada: 'I testify that there is no god but God [Allah], I testify that Muhammad is His messenger'

Crossed swords

COLOUR	PANTONE CODE	CMYK	RGB
	348	100.0.85.24	0.126.72
	355	94.0.100.0	0.155.62
	black 3	60.0.60.91	10.43.26

The JAT logo features two different shades of green. The colour green is associated with the Prophet Muhammad and therefore with Islam itself (see p. 117). Colouring the logo green makes a political statement, as it symbolizes JAT's goal of establishing an Islamic caliphate based on sharia law. This is further emphasized by the inclusion of a variation of the shahada, the Muslim declaration of faith, and a reference to the Sunna and the Qur'an, the holiest books in Islam. The two crossed swords indicate JAT's commitment to jihad. As a pre-modern weapon, the sword is linked to early Islamic jihad campaigns; it is also associated with the purity and nobility of early Islamic heroes. By using swords as a design element JAT confers legitimacy on its jihadi activities, and portrays them as modern extensions of historical jihadi campaigns.

36. JUNDALLAH

Name in Arabic: جند الله

Jundallah (Arabic for 'soldiers of Allah') is an ethno-nationalist Sunni extremist organization; it operates in the Sistan and Baluchistan province of south-eastern Iran and the greater Baluchistan area of Afghanistan and Pakistan. The group was founded in 2003 with the stated goal of defending the rights of the 1.5 million ethnic Baluchis who live under perceived political and cultural oppression as a Sunni minority in Shia-dominated Iran.

Jundallah's founder, Abdulmalik Rigi (who in 2010 was extradited by Pakistan to Iran, where he was executed), stated that violence was a legitimate means of drawing attention to the difficult economic situation and ethnic discrimination of the Baluchi people, and that Jundallah did not have separatist ambitions to create its own state. The group is known for attacks against high-profile Iranian targets, such as government and security officials.

February	2005	Ambush of a motorcade taking the Iranian president, Mahmoud Ahmadinejad, on a visit to Sistan and Baluchistan province, killing 1 of his bodyguards
October	2009	Suicide bombing during a security meeting held by government officials in Pishin, Iran, killing at least 35 people and injuring more than 25
December	2010	Two suicide bombings outside a mosque in Chabahar, Iran, killing 39 people and injuring some 100

Rifle   Crescent moon   Name of group
in Arabic

Book symbolizing
the Qur'an

Raised fist
holding a rifle

COLOUR	PANTONE CODE	CMYK	RGB
	356	95.0.100.27	0.125.50
	1797	0.100.99.4	220.8.20
	012	0.4.100.0	255.231.0
	process black	0.0.0.100	29.29.27

The crescent moon is a symbol of Islamic identity. In Jundallah's logo, the green colour of the crescent evokes the Prophet Muhammad (see p. 117), and thus further highlights the group's commitment to Islam; this makes the crescent a more aggressive, militantly Islamic and fundamentalist symbol than the usually white crescent motif. The raised fist holding a rifle reinforces the group's readiness to use violent means in defence of the interests of Baluchi people and Sunni Muslims. The red outline celebrates the courage of people who fight for their cause, in this case Islam. The open book symbolizes the Qur'an, further emphasizing the group's Islamic ideology. The yellow outline around the book communicates a sense of the divine.

37. KAHANE CHAI / KACH

Name in Hebrew: כהנא חי
Transliteration: kahana hay/kaah

The rabbi Meir Kahane founded the Jewish Defence League (JDL) in 1968 in the United States as an organization dedicated to protecting American Jews from anti-Semitism. In 1969 he emigrated to Israel and established an international office of the JDL. The far-right political party Kach (Hebrew for 'thus' or 'this is the way') emerged from this office.

After Kahane was assassinated in 1990 in New York, his son Binyamin Kahane formed Kahane Chai (Hebrew for 'Kahane lives'). The core leadership of the two groups remained the same, as did the goals – rooted in extremist Jewish ideology – of restoring the biblical land of Israel by annexing all the disputed territories of Israel and forcibly removing all Arabs, and creating a Jewish theocracy.

Kahane Chai operates in Israel, the West Bank and the Gaza Strip. The group is active, and its leaders openly recruit new members and criticize government policy. Its members have threatened violence in response to any Israeli withdrawal from the territories siezed from Egypt, Jordan and Syria during the Six-Day War of 1967.

February	1994	The American-born Kach supporter Baruch Goldstein opens fire in a mosque in Hebron, in the West Bank, killing 29 people and injuring some 150 before being beaten to death by survivors
November	1995	The Kahane Chai member Yigal Amir assassinates the Israeli prime minister, Yitzhak Rabin, in Tel Aviv
March	2002	Time-bomb explosion at an Arab girls' school in Jerusalem, injuring 24 students and 2 teachers

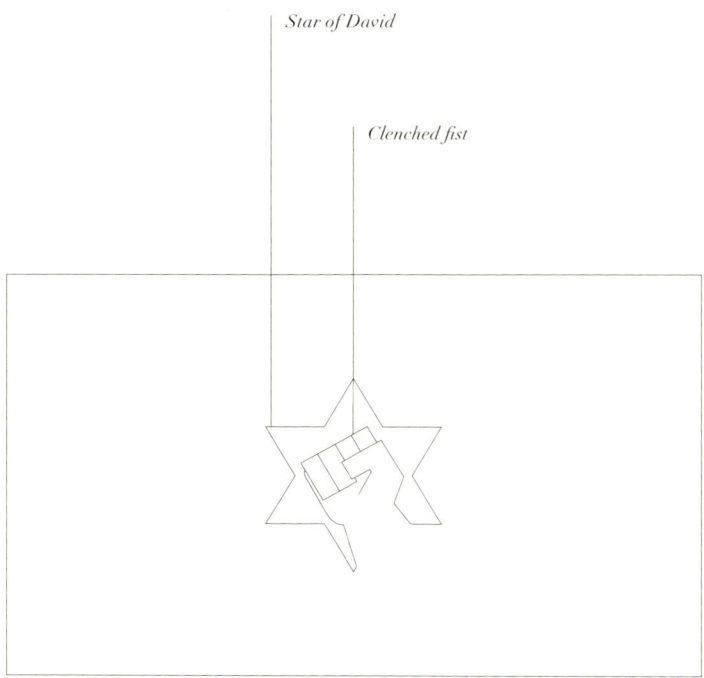

Star of David

Clenched fist

COLOUR	PANTONE CODE	CMYK	RGB
	012	0.4.100.0	255.231.0
	process black	0.0.0.100	0.0.0

The six-pointed Star of David symbolizes Kahane Chai's Jewish identity.
The group's flag has a yellow background; its logo (which appears in
the centre of the flag) sometimes consists of a yellow Star of David
on a black background. The colour yellow is a reminder of the patch
Jews were required to wear in Nazi Germany, and reinforces the group's
Jewish identity and its stated goal of restoring the biblical land of
Israel. The clenched fist conveys courage, strength and militancy. It
illustrates the violent means Kahane Chai is prepared to use in order
to achieve its objectives.

38. KATA'IB HEZBOLLAH (KH)

Name in Arabic: كتائب حزب الله

Kata'ib Hezbollah (Arabic for 'brigades of the party of God'; KH) is a radical Shia Islamist group formed in Iraq in 2006 with the aim of ending American and foreign intervention in Iraq, and of establishing a Shiite Islamic government there. According to the United States government, KH is ideologically tied to Iran and Lebanon-based »Hezbollah, and supported by them. Its 400-odd fighters use classic guerrilla-warfare tactics, including hit-and-run attacks and improvised explosive-device bombings. Targets have included people associated with the United States or other countries that have contributed troops to the multinational forces in Iraq, as well as non-governmental organizations and Iraqi politicians and civilians supportive of the US-initiated political process in Iraq.

KH has concentrated particularly on psychological warfare, recording and distributing video footage of its attacks against American and Coalition soldiers. In 2008 some 1200 videos were seized from a KH media helper, thirty-five of which featured the KH logo.

February	2008	Rocket attack in Baghdad, killing 1 American civilian and injuring several American and Coalition soldiers
November	2008	Rocket attack on the International Zone of Baghdad (also known as the Green Zone), killing 2 United Nations employees
February	2010	Ambush of American and Iraqi military forces entering the village of Duwayjat, Iraq, killing 8 people

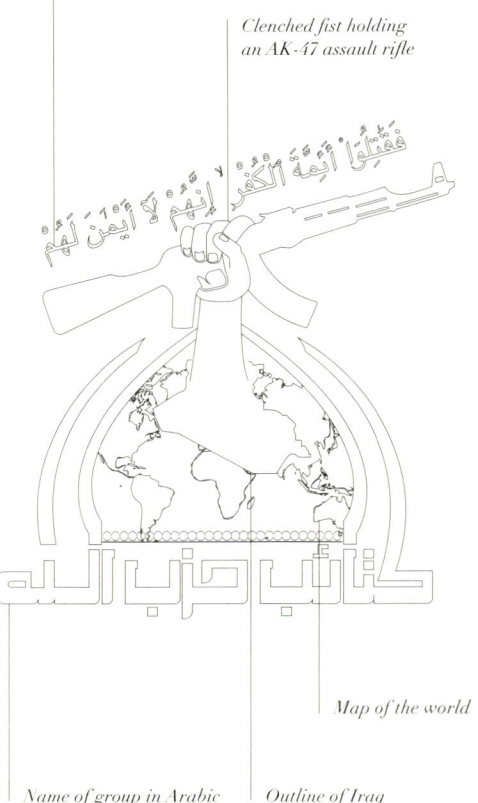

In Arabic, from the Qur'an (9:12): 'Fight the leaders of disbelief, for surely, their oaths are nothing to them'

Clenched fist holding an AK-47 assault rifle

Map of the world

Name of group in Arabic

Outline of Iraq

COLOUR	PANTONE CODE	CMYK	RGB
	180	0.79.100.11	213.75.11
	457	0.15.100.28	200.168.0
	100	0.0.51.0	255.245.153
	process black	0.0.0.100	29.29.27

The map of the world serves as an indication of KH's global aspirations for the Islamic revolution, while the outline of Iraq shows the group's geographical origin and primary operational focus. The maps are contained within a frame in the shape of a mosque dome, which is in turn framed by curved lines resembling swords. The swords are reminders of the violent nature of the group's struggle, and link it to early Islamic history. A rising fist holds an AK-47 assault rifle, a symbol of the group's militancy; a variation of this logo also includes a rocket-propelled grenade (RPG). The rifle portrays KH's struggle as a modern extension of early jihadi campaigns, whereas the RPG exaggerates the military technology available to the group. At the top of the logo is KH's fighting motto, a verse from the Qur'an that speaks about fighting non-believers.

39. KURDISTAN FREEDOM FALCONS (TAK)

Name in Kurdish: Teyrenbaze Azadiya Kurdistan

The Kurdistan Freedom Falcons (more commonly known by its Kurdish-language initials, TAK) is a militant paramilitary Kurdish group operating in Turkey and northern Iraq; it was founded in 2004. The group's goals are not completely clear. It opposes Turkey's 'false policies of the Kurdish issue' and seeks revenge for the deaths of Kurds caused by the Turkish government and military.

Analysts debate whether TAK is a front organization of the »Kurdistan Workers' Party (PKK), but many state that it is a more radical alternative to PKK. The TAK cadre strength is unknown, but is estimated to be only a few dozen active members. The group attacks Turkish and foreign civilians, businesses, and government and legal institutions. It has claimed responsibility for a number of attacks in tourist resorts in Turkey; however, it purports to have no desire to kill foreigners, and wishes only to cut off a key source of revenue for the Turkish government.

June	2005	Bomb explosion in a chemical depot at a bandage factory near Gebze, Turkey, injuring 20 people
February	2006	Bomb explosion in a supermarket in Istanbul, injuring 15 people
February	2006	Bomb explosion in an internet cafe in Istanbul, killing 1 person and injuring 16 others

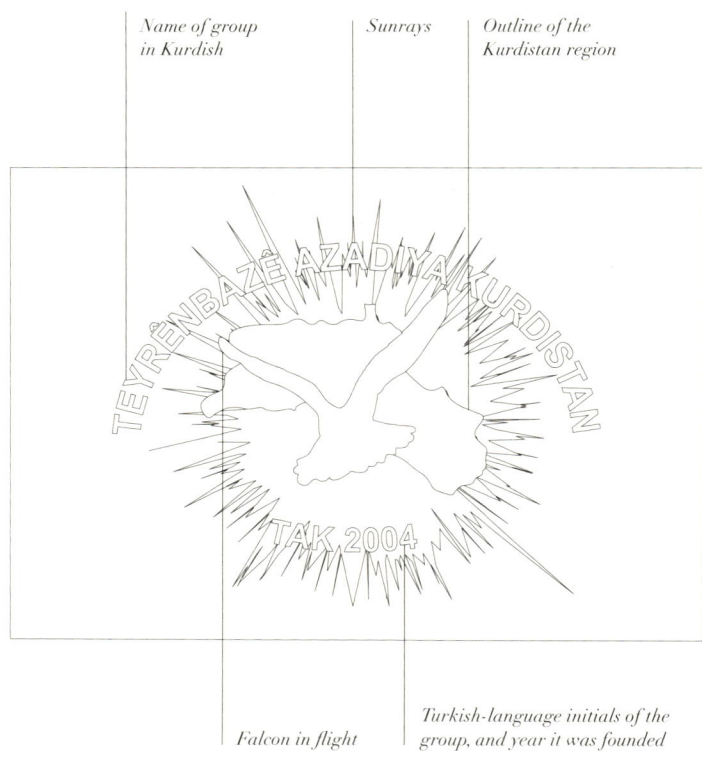

Name of group
in Kurdish

Sunrays

Outline of the
Kurdistan region

Falcon in flight

Turkish-language initials of the
group, and year it was founded

COLOUR	PANTONE CODE	CMYK	RGB
	361	69.0.100.0	86.175.49
	1797	0.100.99.4	220.8.20
	process black	0.0.0.100	0.0.0

The outline of Kurdistan (which encompasses parts of eastern Turkey, northern Iraq, north-western Iran and northern Syria) symbolizes TAK's separatist ambitions for the Kurdish people, while the sunrays reinforce the regional identity of the group. The falcon in flight symbolizes liberty, and more particularly Kurdish freedom; it is also a metaphor for victory, and serves as a promise that the group's struggle will end in triumph.

40. KURDISTAN WORKERS' PARTY (PKK)

Name in Kurdish: Partiya Karkeren Kurdistan

The Kurdistan Workers' Party (better known by its Kurdish-language initials, PKK) was founded in 1978 as a Marxist-Leninist separatist organization with the aim of establishing an independent Kurdish nation in south-eastern Turkey. Today, the PKK calls for autonomy for Kurds within Turkey, and seeks to defend the rights of Kurds, particularly that of maintaining their ethnic identity. By 1999, the year in which its leader, Abdullah Ocalan, was arrested, the group had conducted tens of thousands of attacks; many of these had been large-scale, mass-casualty operations directed at Turkish security forces, Turkish civilians, and tourists, resulting in the deaths of an estimated 30,000-40,000 people.

Following Ocalan's arrest, the PKK announced a unilateral ceasefire, and the organization sought to distance itself from its terrorist past, renaming itself three times. The rebrandings failed, and in 2004 the United States government listed the PKK and its various aliases as terrorist organizations. By 2005 the group had reverted to its original name and called off the ceasefire. The PKK now uses front groups, especially the »Kurdistan Freedom Falcons, to conduct terrorist attacks.

May	2007	Suicide bombing near a market in Ankara, Turkey, killing 10 people and injuring at least 100
January	2008	Car bombing in Diyarbakir, south-eastern Turkey, targets a military bus as it passes a school, killing 6 people and injuring 68
July	2008	Twin bombings in a residential neighbourhood of Istanbul, killing 27 people and injuring more than 150

*Five-pointed star enclosing
a hammer and sickle*

*Burning torch within
a five-pointed star
in a bordered circle*

*Name of group in Kurdish,
and year it was founded*

Sun

*Five-pointed star within
a bordered circle*

COLOUR	PANTONE CODE	CMYK	RGB
	186	0.100.81.4	221.5.43
	116	0.16.100.0	255.211.0
	355	94.0.100.0	0.155.62

Flag of the PKK, used 1978–95

Flag used 1995–2002

Flag used 2003–2005

Flag used since 2005

Each of the PKK's various flags has used the colour red, and most have featured a five-pointed star. The star is commonly used to represent socialism and, in particular, communism; red is the colour of revolution and bloodshed. Together, they illustrate the group's aim of establishing an independent Kurdistan based on Marxist-Leninist principles. The five-pointed star within a circle stands for unity. In the group's first flag, the hammer and sickle, also common communist symbols, underscore the PKK's communist ideology. In the flag used from 1995 to 2002, the burning torch is a symbol of illumination, enlightenment and self-determination; it was later replaced by a sun.

41. LASHKAR-E-TAYYIBA (LET)

Name in Urdu: لشکرطیبہ

Transliteration: leshkər e tejiiba

Lashkar-e-Tayyiba (Urdu for 'army of the pure' or 'army of the righteous'; LET) is a Sunni Islamic extremist organization based in Pakistan. It was launched in about 1990 as the military wing of the political organization Markaz al-Dawa wal-Irshad (Arabic for 'centre for preaching and guidance'). One aim of LET, which positions itself as a missionary and militant organization, is to reshape society and bring the people of Pakistan to its interpretation of Islam through preaching and social welfare. It also aims to wage jihad against India in order to liberate Muslim land that is under perceived Hindu occupation. The group sees jihad as a military obligation for all Muslims, and has recently expanded its involvement in the global jihad.

The hallmark of LET is the so-called fidayeen attack, in which the aim is not to get 'martyred' immediately, but to cause as much damage to the enemy as possible and to inspire fear by fighting to the death. Fidayeen attacks usually entail groups of three to five fighters storming a target and fighting for as long as possible before being overwhelmed; some attacks have lasted more than a day.

August	2003	Twin car bombings in Mumbai, India, killing 52 people and injuring 150
July	2006	Series of 7 bombings on commuter trains in Mumbai, killing more than 209 people and injuring 714
November	2008	Coordinated attacks in Mumbai against a railway station, a restaurant, a hospital, 2 hotels and a Jewish centre, killing 173 people and injuring at least 308

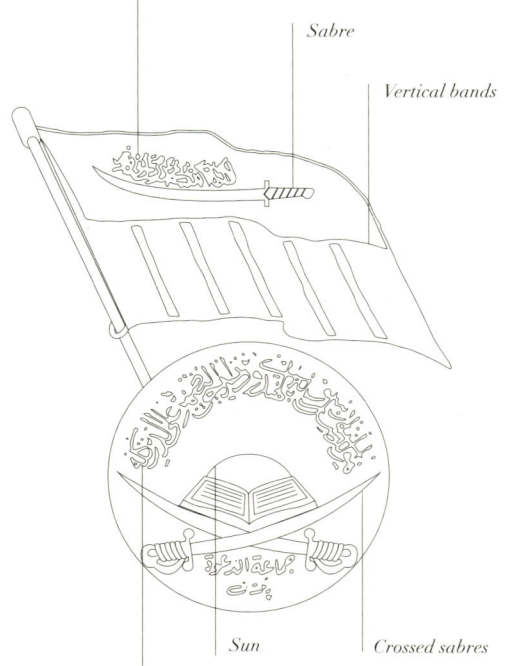

*Flag featuring
the shahada:
'There is no god
but God [Allah],
and Muhammad
is His messenger'*

Sabre

Vertical bands

Sun

Crossed sabres

*In Arabic, from the Qur'an (2:193):
'Fight them until there is no more
tumult or oppression, and there prevail
justice and faith in Allah'*

COLOUR	PANTONE CODE	CMYK	RGB
	1788	0.84.88.0	217.46.30
	123	0.24.94.0	249.168.0
	7511	0.45.100.25	182.109.0
	2935	100.46.0.0	0.92.170
	process black	0.0.0.100	0.0.0

The open Qur'an at the centre of LET's logo is bordered in green, a colour that is associated with the Prophet Muhammad (see p. 117), signifying that Islam is at the heart of the group's ideology. The sun gives the Qur'an a divine character. The commitment of LET to offensive jihad is illustrated by a passage from the Qur'an. Two sabres form a protective frame for the holy book, linking the current jihadi campaign to early Islamic history. (An earlier logo featured an assault rifle rather than sabres.) Above the circular element of the logo flies a black-and-white flag, also featuring a sabre, plus the shahada (the Muslim declaration of faith).

42. LIBERATION TIGERS OF TAMIL EELAM (LTTE)
Name in Tamil: தமிழீழ விடுதலைப் புலிகள்
Transliteration: tamil ila vitutalaip pulika

The Liberation Tigers of Tamil Eelam (LTTE) is a secular nationalist organization based in northern Sri Lanka. It was formed in 1976 with the objective of seizing control of north-eastern Sri Lanka from the Sinhalese (predominantly Buddhist) majority so as to create an independent Tamil state. The Tamils, a mostly Hindu ethnic group, make up 10 per cent of Sri Lanka's population. The cadre strength of the LTTE is approximately 8000. To achieve its goal the group has used both guerrilla tactics and conventional warfare against Sri Lankan military forces and government representatives; targets have also included transport hubs and Buddhist shrines. The conflict has led to the death of some 70,000 people.

The LTTE has a sophisticated structure, being made up of numerous units, each responsible for its own special operations. For example, the Black Tigers unit (see p. 216) is tasked with carrying out suicide bombings, for which it has recruited women and teenagers as well as men. All LTTE fighters wear cyanide capsules around their necks so that they can commit suicide if they are captured. The Sri Lankan government announced the defeat of the group in 2009, and this was conceded by the LTTE.

October	2001	Explosives-laden truck rams a convoy of sailors from the Sri Lankan navy near Habara, killing 100 people and injuring more than 150
January	2007	Truck bombing of the Central Bank of Sri Lanka in Colombo, killing 90 people and injuring more than 1400
June	2008	Detonation of a remote-controlled mine on a bus in Colombo, killing 22 people and injuring more than 50

Ring of bullets

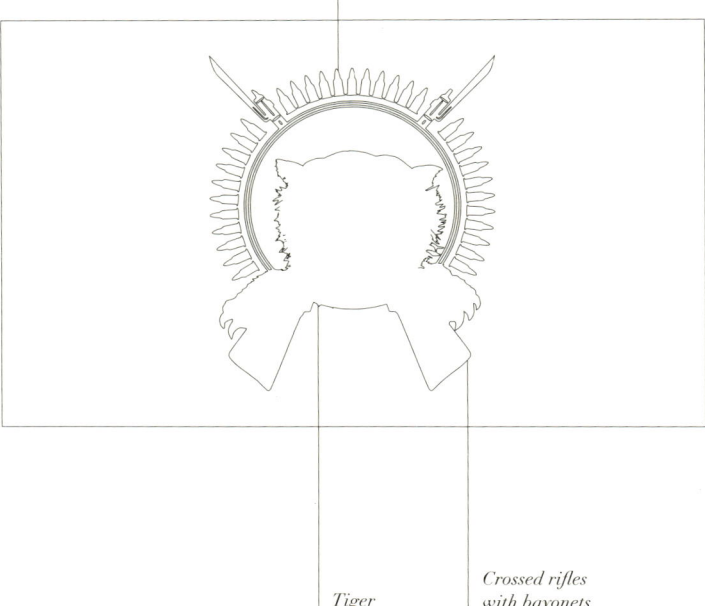

Tiger

*Crossed rifles
with bayonets*

COLOUR	PANTONE CODE	CMYK	RGB
	186	0.100.81.4	221.5.43
	116	0.16.100.0	255.211.0
	process black	0.0.0.100	0.0.0

The yellow roaring tiger on the LTTE flag, and on all the logos of its various units and brigades (see overleaf), is a symbol that is deeply rooted in Tamil culture, symbolizing the martial history and national upheaval of the Tamils. It represents heroism, militancy and patriotism, and emphasizes the group's goal of an independent state. The crossed rifles, and the bullets forming a halo around the tiger, reinforce the militant character of the LTTE. The red of the background can have many meanings, such as revolution and the blood, sacrifice and courage of those who fight for their cause.

Shown opposite are the logos of various LTTE units and brigades.

A. Eela Padai: LTTE's civilian support unit, consisting of civilians responsible
    for guarding homes and fields. The sprig of wheat and AK-47 assault rifle
    signify that the members of this unit are farmers and thus civilians, but are
    ready to take up arms at any time.

B. Black Tigers: the LTTE division tasked with carrying out suicide attacks,
    formed in 1987. The image of a soldier refers to Vallipuram Vasanthan (also
    known as Captain Miller), who carried out LTTE's first suicide attack in
    1987 by driving an explosives-laden truck into a Sri Lanka Army camp, killing
    128 soldiers.

C. Major Sothiya Brigade: one of two LTTE women's wings, named after the first
    female commander and formed in 1989. It carries out both military offensives,
    symbolized by the knife, and administrative tasks, symbolized by the rooster.
    The tree appears only in the imagery of the two women's wings.

D. Malathi Brigade: the other LTTE women's wing, named after the first woman
    killed on behalf of the group, during operations against Indian forces
    performing a peacekeeping operation in Sri Lanka. In common with the other
    women's brigade (above), its logo features a tree.

E. Victor Anti-Tank Battalion: the logo for this unit, formed in 1995, shows two
    crossed rocket-propelled grenade launchers (the unit is said to have had more
    than 350 such weapons in its possession) and a stylized representation of a
    tank track.

F. Charles Anthony Brigade: LTTE's first conventional fighting unit (formed 1991).

G. Sea Tigers: LTTE's naval wing, founded in 1984. Its logo has a blue background
    (for the the sea) and features elements related to ships, such as a ship's
    wheel and an anchor.

H. Air Tigers (or Sky Tigers): the logo of LTTE's airforce shows the tiger and
    a pair of wings on a light blue background. The LTTE is the only terrorist
    organization in the world to have had its own aircraft.

I. Jeyanthan Brigade: consists of fighters from Sri Lanka's Eastern Province. The
    outline map represents the claimed territory; the mermaids symbolize the sea.

A.

B.

C.

D.

E.

F.

G.

H.

I.

43. LIBYAN ISLAMIC FIGHTING GROUP (LIFG)

Name in Arabic: الجماعة الإسلامية المقاتلة بليبيا

Transliteration: al-jama'a al-islamiyyah al-muqatilah bi-Libya

The Libyan Islamic Fighting Group (LIFG) was formed in the early 1990s by Libyan nationals who had fought Soviet forces in Afghanistan. The group's initial objectives were to overthrow the Libyan government run by Muammar Gadcaffi since he had seized power in a military coup in 1969, and to replace it with one based on sharia law. It planned to target Libyan government interests, but remained operationally inactive because many of the LIFG's members fled Libya after the government tightened its security measures. In 2007 »al-Qaeda announced a merger with the LIFG; this was formally disavowed by LIFG members in 2009.

During the Libyan civil war in 2011, the LIFG announced that it had changed its name to the Libyan Islamic Movement (LIM) and declared its support for the revolt against Gaddaffi's government. As LIM, the group has cooperated with the leadership of Libya's National Transitional Council, and has stated that it wants an Islamic government that respects human rights and personal freedom.

May	2003	Suspected of providing materials for suicide bombings in Casablanca, Morocco
July	2009	Announces cessation of terrorist activities in Libya
March	2011	Change of name to Libyan Islamic Movement

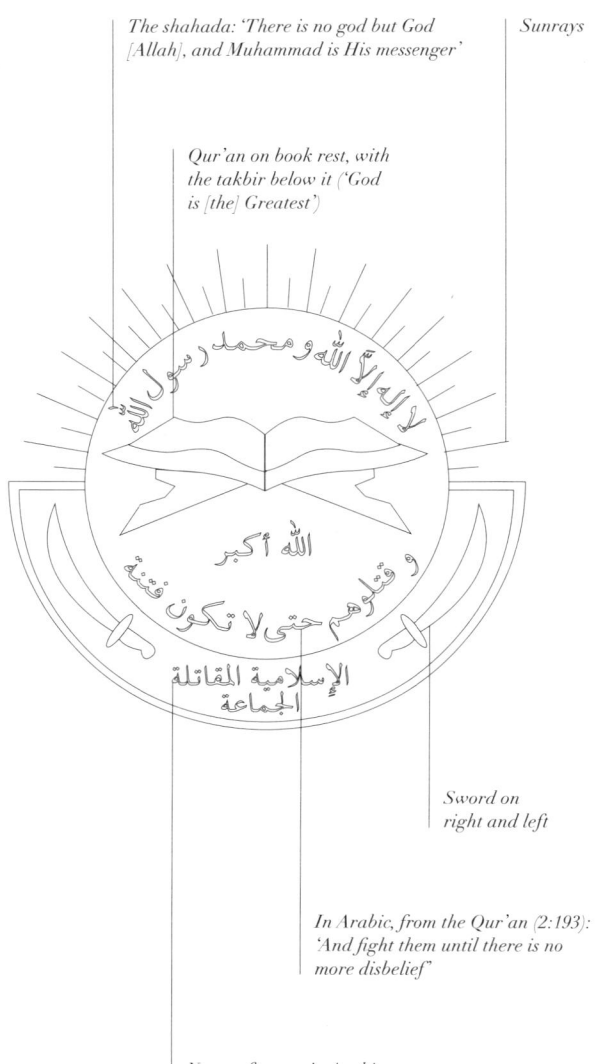

The shahada: 'There is no god but God [Allah], and Muhammad is His messenger'

Sunrays

Qur'an on book rest, with the takbir below it ('God is [the] Greatest')

Sword on right and left

In Arabic, from the Qur'an (2:193): 'And fight them until there is no more disbelief'

Name of group in Arabic

COLOUR	PANTONE CODE	CMYK	RGB
⬛	process black	0.0.0.100	0.0.0

The LIFG logo shows a Qur'an on a book rest, which emphasizes the divine nature of the Qur'an. The shahada (the Muslim declaration of faith) and the takbir (an Arabic phrase translated as 'God is [the] Greatest') are references to the group's religious and political ideologies, which are based on the Qur'an, and thus on Islam. Running in a semicircle below is a passage from the Qur'an that embodies the group's struggle. This struggle, or jihad, is conducted through violent means, which are symbolized by the two swords that form a protective frame for the Qur'an. The swords associate the current jihadi struggle with early Islamic jihadi campaigns. The sunrays add a divine character to the logo, and, by implication, to the LIFG.

44. LOYALIST VOLUNTEER FORCE (LVF)

The Loyalist Volunteer Force (LVF) is a Northern Irish loyalist paramilitary group that was formed in 1997 in a split from the Ulster Volunteer Force, which had a similar ideology but ended its armed campaign in 2007. The LVF seeks to destabilize the Northern Ireland peace process established in 1994, and aims to prevent any union between Northern Ireland and the Republic of Ireland. The group attacks politicians and civilians who support the peace process. It furthermore claims to protect loyalist Protestants from (overwhelmingly Catholic) armed republican groups, such as the »Real Irish Republican Army. The LVF has engaged in bombings, killings and kidnappings in retaliation for attacks by republican groups.

Following the Good Friday Agreement of 1998 (also known as the Belfast Agreement), which instituted the decommissioning of para-military groups' weapons, the LVF declared a ceasefire and began to participate in the disarming process. But, owing to the group's involvement in criminal activities, notably drugs trafficking, the British government has not recognized the ceasefire. After a second ceasefire declaration in 2005, the group's violent attacks decreased. However, reports found in open sources suggest that the LVF remains involved in criminal activities.

November	1999	Machete attack on a Catholic man in Belfast, Northern Ireland, leaving him severly injured
September	2000	Car bombing in Bangor, Northern Ireland, injuring 4 people
October	2000	Killing of the Ulster Volunteer Force commander Richard Jameson in Portadown, Northern Ireland

St George's Cross

_Red Hand of Ulster
with open thumb_

FOR GOD AND ULSTER

COLOUR	PANTONE CODE	CMYK	RGB
	186	0.100.81.4	221.5.43

The Red Hand of Ulster is an ancient heraldic symbol used to denote the Irish province of Ulster, of which six of its nine counties are now part of Northern Ireland; the remaining three are part of the Republic of Ireland. On the LVF flag the Red Hand of Ulster (with open thumb) refers to the group's aim of self-determination and its fight against Irish nationalism. The motto underneath it points to the LVF's roots in religious faith and reinforces its objective of independence from the Republic of Ireland. The inclusion of the St George's Cross, which was the distinguishing mark of English crusaders and now forms the basis of the flag of the United Kingdom, is indicative of the group's loyalty to Britain in the Northern Ireland conflict.

45. MUJAHIDEEN-E-KHALQ ORGANIZATION (MEK)

Name in Persian: سازمان مجاهدین خلق ایران

Transliteration: sazman-e mujahidin-e khalq-e iran

Revolutionary Islam and Marxism inspired the radical student founders of the Mujahideen-e-Khalq Organization (MEK; also known as the People's Mujahideen of Iran). Established in Iran in 1963, the group advocated armed struggle in its opposition to Western influence in Iran and to its country's pro-Western leader, Shah (King) Mohammad Reza Pahlavi. The MEK participated in the Iranian Revolution (1979), which replaced the shah with a Shiite Islamic regime led by Ayatollah Khomeini. However, the group's ideology – a mixture of Marxism, feminism and Islamism – was at odds with the new regime. In 1981, following the execution of most of the MEK leadership by the government, the group moved its base to Paris, from where it supported Iraq's war against Iran (1980-88). It resettled in Iraq in 1986; since 2003, it has been based mainly at Camp Ashraf, a refugee camp north of Baghdad.

The MEK has some 3400 members, and its commando corps is composed mostly of women. It remains the strongest armed opposition to the clerical Iranian regime. Ideologically led by the husband-and-wife duo Massoud and Maryam Rajavi, the organization advocates a secular, democratic government. It aims to overthrow the Iranian regime through its military wing, the National Liberation Army, and its political front, the National Council of Resistance of Iran.

June	1981	Bombing of the head office of the ruling Islamic Republic Party in Tehran, Iran, killing 70 officials, including the president, Mohammad Ali Rajai
February	2000	Mortar attack on the presidential palace in Tehran, killing 1 person and injuring 4 others
September	2012	The MEK is removed from the United States' list of designated foreign terrorist groups

Globe

Outline
of Iran

Five-
pointed
red star

In Arabic, from the Qur'an (4:95): 'To
each, Allah has promised good Paradise,
but Allah has preferred those who strive
hard and fight, above those who sit [at
home] with a huge reward'

Scythe

Sprig of wheat

The Arabic word mujahid, from
which rises a fist holding a rifle

Anvil

Name of group in Persian

COLOUR	PANTONE CODE	CMYK	RGB
	1797	0.100.99.4	220.8.20

At the centre of the MEK logo is an outline of Iran, showing the origin and identity of the group, as well as the main territory of its operations. The five-pointed star above it is a reference to Marxism. Both the map and the star are enclosed in a representation of the globe, symbolizing the global ambitions of the Marxist and Islamic revolutions. The anvil at the bottom represents the worker; above it is the word 'mujahid', from which emerges a clenched fist holding a rifle, representing the soldier and the MEK's commitment to armed struggle. The scythe refers to the farmer, and the sprig of wheat symbolizes prosperity.

Huma bird

Five-pointed star

Sprigs of wheat

اوتی آزادیبخش ملی ایران

Name of group in Persian

The year the group was founded: 1366 (Jalali or Persian calendar; 1987 in the Gregorian or Western calendar)

COLOUR	PANTONE CODE	CMYK	RGB
	279	68.34.0.0	86.146.206
	process yellow	0.0.100.0	255.237.0

The flag of the MEK's military wing, the National Liberation Army
(NLA), features the huma, a legendary bird of Iranian mythology that
spent its whole life on the wing. It is the bird both of paradise and
of fortune, and has both male and female characteristics. Its inclusion is indicative of the NLA's commitment to the struggle of men and
women alike. The sprigs of wheat symbolize prosperity for the democratic government of Iran that the MEK's endeavours will bring about.

46. MUSLIM BROTHERHOOD (MB)

Name in Arabic: الإخوان المسلمون

Transliteration: al-ihwan al-muslimun

The Sunni organization Muslim Brotherhood (MB) was founded in Egypt in 1928 by the Islamic scholar Hassan al-Banna. Its initial goal was the overthrow of Egypt's monarchy (achieved by the Free Officers Movement in 1952) and its replacement by a government based on sharia law. The group's motto, quoted on numerous websites, is 'Allah is our objective. The Prophet is our leader. Qur'an is our law. Jihad is our way. Dying in the way of Allah is our highest hope.' This illustrates the MB's devotion to Islam and jihad in order to advance Islam's global conquest; to establish an Islamic caliphate; and to spread a sense of duty to wage jihad to reclaim territory perceived to be occupied by Israel. Over the years the MB has established branches in more than seventy countries.

In the late 1970s the MB began to distance itself from its violent past, and to build a reputation as a moderate and reformist organization. It now pursues its goals not only through acts of violence but also through ideological influence on other groups. It also participates in local and national politics in various countries; for example, MB members sit in the Jordanian parliament, dominate the Egyptian parliament and control the Syrian opposition in exile.

December	1948	Assassination of the Egyptian prime minister, Mahmud Fahmi Nuqrashi, who had banned the MB
October	1981	Participation in the assassination of the Egyptian president, Anwar al-Sadat
February	2012	The leader of MB's Jordanian branch, Hammad Said, states that jihad against the Syrian president, Bashar al-Assad, is an Islamic duty

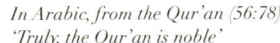
In Arabic, from the Qur'an (56:78):
'Truly, the Qur'an is noble'

Crossed swords.
Below them, in Arabic, from
the Qur'an (8:60): 'Be prepared!'

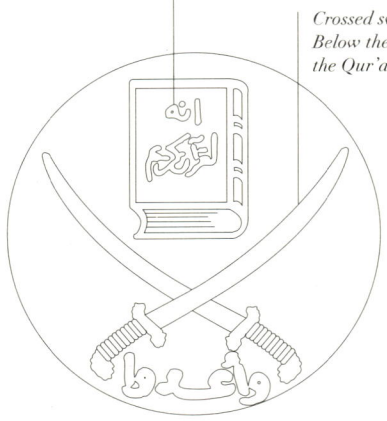

In Arabic:
'The Qur'an is noble'

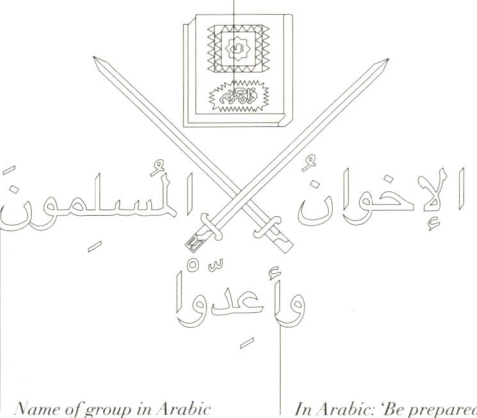

Name of group in Arabic

In Arabic: 'Be prepared!'

COLOUR	PANTONE CODE	CMYK	RGB
	1797	0.100.99.4	220.8.20
	355	94.0.100.0	0.155.62
	process black	0.0.0.100	0.0.0

Logo of the MB

Variation of the MB logo

On both versions of the MB logo, the Qur'an, labelled as 'noble', represents the group's strong ideological foundation in Islam. The two crossed swords illustrate the group's commitment to militant jihad in order to realize its aims; as pre-modern weapons, they confer historical legitimacy on jihad and evoke notions of historic Islam. Beneath the swords is the Arabic for 'be prepared', a reference to a verse from the Qur'an in which the reader is urged to him- or herself to fight the 'enemy of Allah'. The variation of the standard logo also features the group's name running across it.

47. NATIONAL DEMOCRATIC FRONT OF BODOLAND (NDFB)

The Bodo are an ethnic people of India, based in the state of Assam, where they form about 10 per cent of the local population; most Bodo are either Hindu or Christian. The objective of the National Democratic Front of Bodoland (NDFB), formed in 1988 under the name Bodo Security Force and renamed the NDFB in 1994, is to create a fully independent nation, Bodoland. It also believes that the Bodo language should be written in Roman script and not in the Devanagari script that is used for standard Hindi. It has some 1500 members.

The NDFB has committed acts of insurgency, attacking targets representing the Indian government and the non-Bodo civilian population. Acts ascribed to the group include murders, bombings and kidnappings for ransom. In 2011 the NDFB announced an indefinite ceasefire in order to pave the way for negotiations with the Indian government.

November	1992	Bombing of a bus in Guwahati, in the Indian state of Assam, killing 38 people and injuring 20
October	2004	Bombings of the main train station and a market in Dimapur, in the Indian state of Nagaland, killing more than 20 people and injuring 40
November	2010	Firearm attack on a public bus in Sonitpor, Assam, targeting government employees and Hindi speakers, killing 8 people and injuring 12

Five-pointed star within a circle

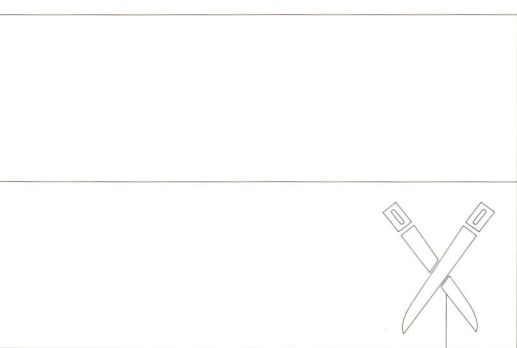

Crossed objects, possibly bladed weapons

COLOUR	PANTONE CODE	CMYK	RGB
	355	94.0.100.0	0.155.62
	186	0.100.81.4	221.5.43
	process yellow	0.0.100.0	255.237.0

Very little detail is available about the imagery used by the NDFB. Reports in open sources suggest that its green flag, featuring a yellow five-pointed star in a red circle, is the ethnic flag of the Bodo people, and would be chosen by the NDFB as the official national flag of an independent Bodoland. Reports also state that the red and yellow flag, featuring two unidentified objects that may be bladed implements, has been used by NDFB militants.

48. NATIONAL LIBERATION ARMY (ELN)

Name in Spanish: Ejército de Liberación Nacional

The National Liberation Army (commonly referred to by its Spanish-language initials, ELN) is a Colombian nationalist guerrilla movement founded in 1964. It is inspired by Marxist-Leninist ideology, liberation theology, the Cuban revolution (1953-59) and the mid-twentieth-century Latin American Marxist revolutionary Che Guevara. The group claims to represent the rural poor in their struggle against Colombia's wealthy classes, and opposes American involvement in Colombia, the privatization of natural resources, multinational corporations and right-wing militant groups.

The ELN operates mainly in north-eastern Colombia; it is estimated to have some 2000 armed combatants, with an unknown number of additional active supporters. The group has a centralized command-and-control structure, and operates through so-called 'war fronts' based in several major cities and various villages. It conducts bombing campaigns and extortion against domestic and multinational companies, as well as kidnappings for ransom, hijackings and attacks against oil-industry infrastructure. The ELN has also been accused of being involved in the drugs trade and of cooperating with criminal gangs.

March	2003	Bomb explosion in an underground car park at a shopping centre in Cúcuta, Colombia, killing 7 people and injuring 68
May	2008	Open letter to the secretariat of the »Revolutionary Armed Forces of Colombia, seeking cooperation in the struggle
June	2010	Attack near Tibu, Colombia, killing 7 police officers

In Spanish: 'Not one step
backwards, Liberation or death'

Rifle   Hammer and machete

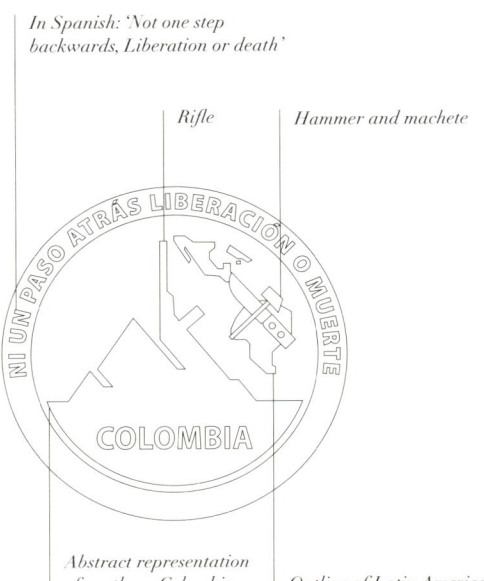

Abstract representation
of northern Colombia   Outline of Latin America

Initials of the group's name in Spanish

COLOUR	PANTONE CODE	CMYK	RGB
	1797	0.100.99.4	220.8.20
	process black	0.0.0.100	0.0.0

Logo of the ELN

Flag of the ELN

The ELN website states that the colour red in the group's logo and flag symbolizes freedom and the blood that has been shed in the struggle for the revolution; black stands for the mourning of those killed during the struggle. Both colours are used by communists and revolutionaries around the world, and therefore here represent the ELN's internationalist position. The colour white used for the lettering represents a commitment to peace.

The circular shape of the ELN logo symbolizes unity. The group's geographical location is illustrated by an abstract representation of northern Colombia, showing the valleys of the rivers Cauca and Magdalena. The rifle represents the armed struggle that emerges from the area's mountains. The outline of Latin America, to the right of the rifle, symbolizes the continent-wide fight of the group. The hammer and machete represent the working class and the peasantry, which form its main supporters and member base.

49. NATIONAL LIBERATION FRONT OF TRIPURA (NLFT)

The National Liberation Front of Tripura (NLFT), founded in 1989, is a separatist militant group operating in the Indian state of Tripura. It advocates the furtherance of Tripuri tribal identity, and its objective is the establishment of an independent Tripuri nation. Dispatches in open sources, such as reports by the BBC, suggest that it has some 1500 members, aproximately 90 per cent of whom are Christian, and that it is partly funded by the Tripura Baptist Christian Union. In 2001 an NLFT statement urged all Tripura citizens to become Christians. The NLFT engages in terrorist activities against non-Tripuri people and representatives of the Indian government, using knives, firearms and mines.

March	2001	Ambush of a police patrol in Bampu, southern Tripura, killing 13 people
December	2002	Shooting in a market in Tripura, killing 12 people and injuring 13
October	2009	Kidnapping of 8 people in Kusharambai, Tripura; all are killed

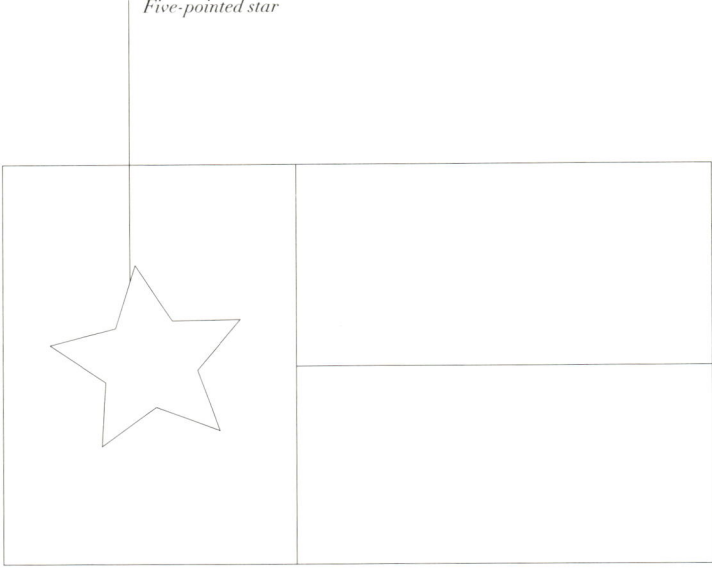

Five-pointed star

COLOUR	PANTONE CODE	CMYK	RGB
	355	94.0.100.0	0.155.62
	186	0.100.81.4	221.5.43

The constitution of the NLFT explains that the white five-pointed star on its flag is the guiding star for all Tripuri tribes. The colour green symbolizes the sovereignty of the land on which the tribes live. Red represents the revolution that is necessary to achieve the goal of an independent Tripura, and suggests the bloodshed that may result from the struggle for independence. White stands for peace; the NLFT relate this to both the peace-loving people of Tripura and the peaceful means that can assist in the struggle for independence.

50. ORANGE VOLUNTEERS (OV)

The Orange Volunteers (OV) is a loyalist paramilitary organization operating in Northern Ireland. It was founded in 1998 and has fewer than 25 members. Its objective is to maintain British rule in Northern Ireland; it is therefore believed that the group was established for the purpose of destabilizing the Good Friday Agreement (also known as the Belfast Agreement) of 1998, which redefines the relationship between Northern Ireland and both the Republic of Ireland and the United Kingdom. The OV furthermore claims that it has a duty to protect Northern Ireland's Protestant population from threats by Catholic republicans, as well as to protect the Protestant faith as a whole.

The OV engages in pipe bombings, arson attacks and physical assaults, targeting Catholic churches, businesses and civilians. Several leading members were arrested in 1999, and in 2000 the group declared a ceasefire, but violent activities continued. A second ceasefire was proclaimed in 2001. In 2003 the group demonstrated its strength with photographs of volunteers training with new handguns, an assault rifle and a silencer, and threatened to end the ceasefire with catholic paramilitary groups if an unsatisfactory peace deal was agreed. In the years since, the OV has continued to have attacks ascribed to it.

September	1999	Explosive-device attack on a bar in Nutts Corner, near Belfast, Northern Ireland, injuring 1 person
November	2005	Participation in a 2-night riot in Belfast and nearby towns, injuring some 50 police officers
August	2009	Pipe-bomb explosion in Dungannon, Northern Ireland, damaging a van but causing no casualties

St Andrew's Cross

Flag of the defunct Government
of Northern Ireland (1953–72)

Crossed
rifles

Crown

Latin proverb at bottom and in
centre: 'Fortune favours the brave'

To left and right:
Year the group
was founded

Five-pointed star featuring the
Red Hand of Ulster (thumb open)

COLOUR	PANTONE CODE	CMYK	RGB
	186	0.100.81.4	221.5.43
	116	0.16.100.0	255.211.0
	7442	50.70.0.0	149.96.164
	072	100.88.0.5	36.53.136
	7510	0.30.72.11	230.175.82
	process black	0.0.0.100	0.0.0

The OV logo proclaims the year in which the group was founded (1998) and features two flags. The one on the left is a St Andrew's Cross, a reference to Scottish loyalist Protestants during the eighteenth-century Jacobite rebellions in Scotland. The flag on the right, with an orange cross, was that of the defunct Government of Northern Ireland, which ruled from 1953 until the Northern Ireland parliament was dissolved by the British government in 1972. The colour orange refers to the Protestant William III of Orange, who at the Battle of the Boyne (1690) defeated the Catholic James II (who had been attempting to regain the thrones of England, Scotland and Ireland), thus securing religious freedom for the Protestants of Northern Ireland. The purple star, a symbol of Williamite forces, and the crossed rifles refer to this battle and portray the OV's current struggle as an extension of William's campaign. The crown symbolizes the group's loyalty to the British crown.

51. PALESTINE LIBERATION FRONT (PLF)

Name in Arabic: جبهة التحرير الفلسطينية

Transliteration: dschaɔhat at-tahrir al-filastiniyya

The Palestine Liberction Front (PLF) was founded as a secular Marxist organization by Ahmed Jibril, a former captain of the Syrian army, in 1959, with a view tc liberating Palestinian territory from perceived Israeli occupation. In 1967 the group merged with two others to form the »Popular Front for the Liberation of Palestine (PFLP); this split the following year, leading to the formation of the »PFLP-General Command. That group's pro-Syrian stance led Muhammad Zaidan (also known as Abu Addas) to re-establish the PLF in 1977.

Zaidan's Tunisia-based PLF section has had close ties with the Palestine Liberation Organization (PLO), a paramilitary and political organization formed in 1964 and now recognized by the United Nations and 100 nation states as the sole legitimate representative of the Palestinian people. The PLF supported the signing of the 1993 Oslo Accord between the government of Israel and the PLO; it recognized Israel and officially renounced terrorism against that country. The group took part in the Palestinian elections of 2006 but did not win a seat. After almosⴢ sixteen years without an attack, in 2008 the PLF claimed responsibility for two attacks against Israeli targets. A PLF Central Committee member then reiterated the group's commitment to the Palestinian 'struggle' and 'resistance' through its military wing.

April	1979	PLF members enter Israel by boat from Lebanon and raid the coastal city of Nahariya, killing 4 people
October	1985	Hijacking of the Italian cruise ship Achille Lauro, murdering and throwing overboard the wheelchair-bound Jewish American citizen Leon Klinghoffer
March	2008	Gunshot wounding of an Israeli settler south of the Hebron Hills

Outline of
Palestine

Five-pointed star

Gun barrel

Name of group in Arabic

COLOUR	PANTONE CODE	CMYK	RGB
	355	94.0.100.0	0.155.62
	186	0.100.81.4	221.5.43
	process black	0.0.0.100	0.0.0

The PLF logo is in the colours of the Palestinian flag (red, black, white and green), evoking Palestinian nationalism. The red five-pointed star symbolizes the group's Marxist ideology. The outline of Palestine denotes the objective of freeing the territory from perceived Israeli occupation. The gun barrel stands for armed struggle, and symbolizes the group's commitment to violent means in order to achieve its aims. Some sources claim that the semicircular shape on the right represents a crescent moon, but this is unlikely given the PLF's Marxist (rather than Islamist) ideology.

52. PEOPLE'S LIBERATION ARMY (PLA)

The People's Liberation Army (PLA) was formed in 1978 with the objective of 'liberating' Manipur, a state of north-eastern India, from perceived Indian occupation. Its strategy involved setting up a revolutionary front that would unite all dissenting ethnic groups and tribes in India's north-east.

Estimates for the PLA's current cadre strength range between 1500 and 3000. The group has engaged in a guerrilla insurgency campaign against the Indian government, targeting law-enforcement personnel and military and security forces within Manipur and along its border regions. It maintains a large supply of firearms; reports by some analysts suggest that it has the potential to create explosive devices.

In 1979 the PLA formed a political wing, the Revolutionary People's Front (RPF), which currently runs a government in exile from Bangladesh. Among other things, the RPF engages in social vigilantism. For example, in 1996 it created a task force, known as 'STAFORCE', designed to combat drug addiction and the spread of HIV and AIDS, control perceived immoral behaviour and curb political corruption; this campaign involved aggressive enforcement by PLA militants.

March	1984	Attack on a paramilitary patrol in Imphal, Manipur, killing 14 people and injuring 40
February	1989	Attack on Indian police officials in Imphal, killing 5 people
January	1997	Armed assault on Indian government officials in Vingthoukom, Manipur, killing 6 people and injuring 5

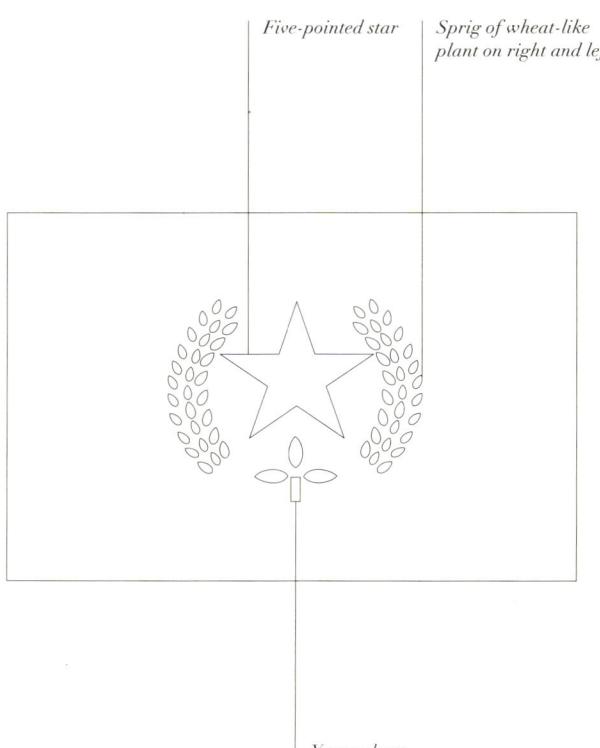

Five-pointed star

Sprig of wheat-like
plant on right and left

Young shoot

COLOUR	PANTONE CODE	CMYK	RGB
	1797	0.100.99.4	220.8.20
	116	0.16.100.0	255.211.0
	355	94.0.100.0	0.155.62

The red flag symbolizes the revolution the PLA aims to achieve in Manipur. The yellow five-pointed star at the centre represents the unity of all ethnic tribes involved in the fight against perceived Indian occupation. ⁻he sprigs of wheat-like plants on either side represent the group's promise to create an independent state, and symbolize eventual victcry. The young green shoot at the bottom represents the beginning of a new nation state, which will live in prosperity.

53. POPULAR FRONT FOR THE LIBERATION OF PALESTINE (PFLP)

Name in Arabic: الجبهة الشعبية لتحرير فلسطين

Transliteration: al-jabha al-sha'biyyah li-tahir filastin

The Popular Front for the Liberation of Palestine (PFLP) is a Marxist-Leninist, secular, nationalist Palestinian movement. It was founded by the Palestinian Christian doctor George Habash after the defeat by Israel of the pan-Arab movement during the Six-Day War of 1967. The PFLP focuses its attention on Palestinian nationalism, and sees the 'liberation' of Palestine from perceived Israeli occupation as an integral part of a global communist revolution. It is opposed to any sort of peace process, and favours a one-state solution that would destroy Israel. After Fatah, the secular nationalist movement formed by Yasser Arafat, the PFLP is the second largest of the groups forming the Palestine Liberation Organization (PLO; see p. 253). It set up a military wing, the Abu Ali Mustafa Brigades, in 2001.

In 1968 the PFLP was one of the first terrorist organizations to engage in the armed hijacking of aeroplanes, when it succeeded in diverting to Algeria a commercial airliner flying from Italy to Israel. No passengers or crew were killed, but some were kept as hostages for more than five weeks, until the Israeli government agreed to an exchange of prisoners. The group currently engages predominantly in suicide bombings against Israeli civilians.

September	1970	Hijacking of 4 commercial airliners (3 departing from European airports, 1 from Bahrain), diverting them to Jordan and blowing them up after evacuating the hostages
October	2001	Assassination of the Israeli tourism minister, Rehavam Ze'evi, in a hotel in Jerusalem
November	2004	Suicide bombing in a market in Tel Aviv, killing 3 people and wounding more than 30

Arrow (and dot below) in the
form of the Arabic letter 'jeem'

Outline of Palestine

COLOUR	PANTONE CODE	CMYK	RGB
■	1797	0.100.99.4	220.8.20

Logo of the PFLP

Flag of the PFLP

The red colour of the PFLP logo and flag hints at the group's Marxist-inspired ideology. In the left half of the logo is an outline of Palestine; on the flag, colouring this in red makes the political statement that the government of Palestine should be based on communist principles. Red also symbolizes bloodshed and war, and indicates the PFLP's commitment to armed struggle in order to realize its aims. The arrow pointing towards Palestine is in the shape of the Arabic letter 'jeem, the first letter of the word <u>jabha</u>, Arabic for 'front'. Its placement outside Palestine indicates the PFLP's support from non-Palestinian insurgent groups, such as the German left-wing guerrilla group Rote Armee Faktion, which was dissolved in 1998 but was a major supporter when the PFLP was founded (see also p. 125).

Name of group in Arabic   Palestinian flag in the background

AK-47 assault rifle

COLOUR	PANTONE CODE	CMYK	RGB
	186	0.100.81.4	221.5.43
	356	95.0.100.27	0.125.50
	process black	0.0.0.100	0.0.0

The logo of the PFLP's military wing, the Abu Ali Mustafa Brigades, is based on the main group's logo, but its background also features a faint representation of the Palestinian flag, which reinforces the message that the group favours Palestinian nationalism. The dark background and the image of the AK-47 assault rifle stand for militarism and armed struggle.

Pattern module A
Four solid rectangles linked by thin lines; a section containing repeats of this pattern module forms the centre of the keffiyeh.

Pattern module B
A rounded and symmetrical wave shape; repeats of this pattern module form the borders of the keffiyeh.

Pattern module C
A main rectangular band, flanked on either side by a thinner line; this pattern is sometimes overlaid at right angles on another similar pattern, creating crossing points with a transparency effect. These bands separate pattern modules A and B.

The keffiyeh is a traditional headdress worn by Arab men, consisting of a square of cloth, usually made of cotton, that is folded and wrapped in various ways around the head. Patterns and colours vary according to the country; the traditional Palestinian pattern is shown opposite. During the mid- to late 1930s, the keffiyeh, worn by Palestinian demonstrators protesting against British occupation, became a symbol of Palestinian nationalism. The colour of the pattern is associated with the political sympathies of the wearer; red-and-white keffiyehs have been used by Marxist groups, such as the PFLP. Today, this colour is also chosen by supporters and members of »Hamas.

Keffiyeh pattern favoured by PFLP militants

54. POPULAR FRONT FOR THE LIBERATION OF PALESTINE – GENERAL COMMAND (PFLP-GC)

Name in Arabic: الجبهة الشعبية لتحرير فلسطين - القيادة العامة

Transliteration: al-jabha al-sha'biyya li-tahir filastin - al-qiyada al-ammah

The Popular Front for the Liberation of Palestine – General Command (PFLP-GC) was founded in 1968 as a Syrian-backed splinter group of the secular Marxist »Popular Front for the Liberation of Palestine, claiming that it wanted to focus more on fighting to 'liberate' Palestine from perceived Israeli occupation and less on political efforts. The group was originally violently opposed to the Arafat-led Palestine Liberation Organization, which signed the Oslo Accord with Israel in 1993 (see also »Palestine Liberation Front). The PFLP-GC is headed by Ahmed Jibril, a former captain of the Syrian army who has close ties with Syria and Iran, and has a cadre strength of between several hundred and several thousand. It maintains an armed presence in Palestinian refugee camps in Syria, and has its own military bases in Lebanon and along the Lebanon-Syria border.

The PFLP-GC is known for cross-border attacks against Israel by unusual means, such as hot-air balloons and microlights. In recent years the group has focused primarily on supporting »Hezbollah's attacks against Israel, training members of other Palestinian militant groups, and smuggling weapons.

November	2007	Militant flies a hang-glider into an Israeli army camp near the Lebanese border, killing 6 people and wounding several others before being shot dead
May	2008	Rocket attack on a shopping centre in Ashkelon, Israel, wounding at least 10 people
March	2010	Rocket attack on an Israeli military base, causing no injuries or damage

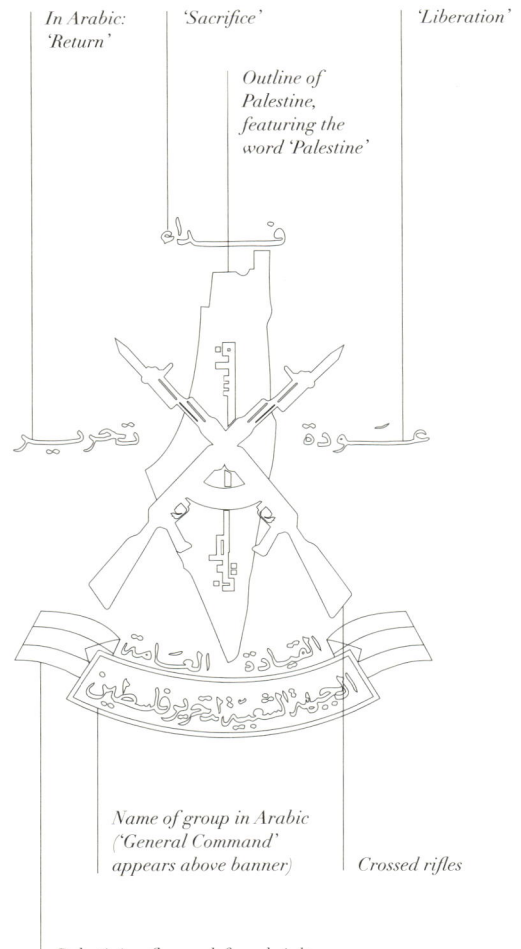

In Arabic:
'Return'

'Sacrifice'

'Liberation'

Outline of
Palestine,
featuring the
word 'Palestine'

قدس

عودة

تحرير

القيادة العامة

الجبهة الشعبية لتحرير فلسطين

Name of group in Arabic
('General Command'
appears above banner)

Crossed rifles

Palestinian flag on left and right

COLOUR	PANTONE CODE	CMYK	RGB
	356	95.0.100.27	0.120.44
	185	0.91.76.0	227.35.51
	process black	0.0.0.100	0.0.0

The PFLP-GC logo is in the colours of the Palestinian flag (which appears twice at the bottom of the logo): red, black, white and green. The flag, together with the outline of Palestine, symbolizes the group's nationalism and its objective of liberating Palestine from perceived occupation by Israel. The three words 'liberation', 'sacrifice' and 'return' form the slogan of the group and reinforce its aims. 'Return' refers to the desire of Palestinian refugees to return to their homeland and reflects the fact that the group was founded in a refugee camp. 'Sacrifice' refers to martyrdom and indicates that the group's members are prepared to die for their cause. The crossed assault rifles stand for the group's militant nature and its readiness to use armed struggle to achieve its goals.

Popular Front for the Liberation of Palestine – General Command (PFLP-GC)

55. REAL IRISH REPUBLICAN ARMY (REAL IRA)

The Real Irish Republican Army (Real IRA) is an Irish republican paramilitary organization formed by Michael McKevitt and his common-law wife Bernadette Sands-McKevitt in Northern Ireland in 1997, after the Provisional IRA (usually referred to simply as the IRA) had endorsed the Northern Ireland peace process. The Real IRA objects to the division of Ireland into a southern independent republic and a northern region that is part of the United Kingdom, and its objective is to end British sovereignty over Northern Ireland through the use of force.

The Real IRA's main power base is in the border towns of Dundalk (Republic of Ireland) and Newry (Northern Ireland). Its Army Council plans and directs terrorist operations; rank-and-file members operate in covert cells. In addition, the group has a political wing, the 32 County Sovereignty Movement. The Real IRA has been responsible for a number of bombings in Northern Ireland and England of commercial and civilian targets. Weapons include home-made mortars and landmines. In 2003 McKevitt was sentenced to twenty years' imprisonment for directing terrorism; the Real IRA has since regrouped and continues to be active, both in the United Kingdom and in the Republic of Ireland.

| August | 1998 | Car bomb in Omagh, Northern Ireland, killing 29 people and injuring some 220 |
| June | 2000 | Bomb explosion on Hammersmith Bridge in London, causing slight damage |

*Tricolor flag of
the Irish Republic*

COLOUR	PANTONE CODE	CMYK	RGB
	347	100.0.86.3	0.148.83
	151	0.48.95.0	244.151.18

The Real IRA has used the tricolour flag of the Irish Republic in many of it murals. In symbolism that dates back to the late eighteenth-century Society of United Irishmen, green represents Irish republicanism. Orange represents the minority of Irishmen who supported William III, Protestant king of England, Scotland and Ireland, who defeated the deposed James II, a Catholic, and his predominantly Irish Catholic army at the Battle of the Boyne in 1690. Placed between these two colours, white signifies a lasting truce between the two cultures (Irish Catholic and Irish Protestant) and peaceful coexistence.

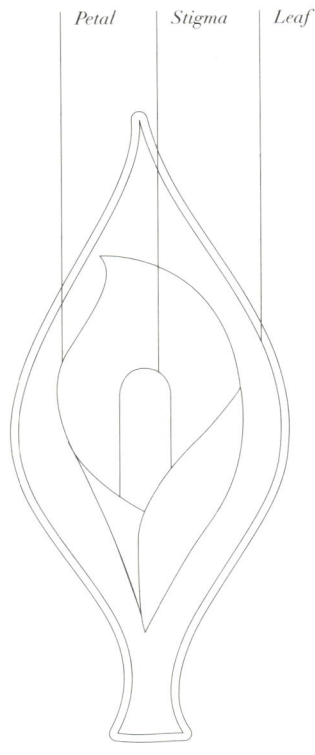

Petal   Stigma   Leaf

COLOUR	PANTONE CODE	CMYK	RGB
■	5535	66.0.57.82	17.60.43
■	151	0.48.95.0	244.151.18
■	8580	31.50.75.28	150.110.64

During Easter week in 1916, a group of Irish republicans started an insurgence against British rule that achieved the seizure of key locations in Dublin and the proclamation of an Irish Republic. At the time of the insurgency, the Easter lily was being used as decoration in churches; today, the Easter lily badge is worn by Irish republicans as a symbol of remembrance for those who have died fighting for Irish independence.

56. REVOLUTIONARY ARMED FORCES OF COLOMBIA (FARC)

Name in Spanish: Fuerzas Armadas Revolucionarias de Colombia -
Ejército del Pueblo

The Revolutionary Armed Forces of Colombia (more commonly known by its Spanish-language acronym, FARC) has its roots in the peasant insurgency in Colombia that took place during the 1920s and 1930s. In 1958 the country's two main political parties agreed to share power in exclusion of others; this led, in 1964, to the founding of FARC, a militant left-wing Marxist organization, by communist militants and peasant self-defence groups. The organization claims to represent the rural poor in a struggle against the wealthy elite; it opposes American influence in Colombia, the privatization of natural resources, multinational corporations and right-wing paramilitary organizations.

At its height in the early years of the twenty-first century, FARC had approximately 17,000 fighters and controlled one third of Colombia. An aggressive US-backed counter-insurgency by Colombian forces (dubbed Operation Espada de Honor, Spanish for 'sword of honour') has driven the group back to more remote regions; by 2010 its strength had been reduced to some 8000 fighters. FARC's foremost tactic is kidnapping wealthy landowners, tourists, and international and domestic officials. In 2012 the group announced that it would no longer take hostages for ransom.

February	2002	Kidnapping of the Colombian presidential candidate Ingrid Betancourt, who was travelling in guerrilla territory; she is rescued, along with 14 other hostages, in 2008
February	2002	Hijacking of a domestic commercial flight, and kidnapping of a Colombian senator on board
November	2005	Kidnapping of 60 people, to exchange them for FARC members detained in Colombian prisons

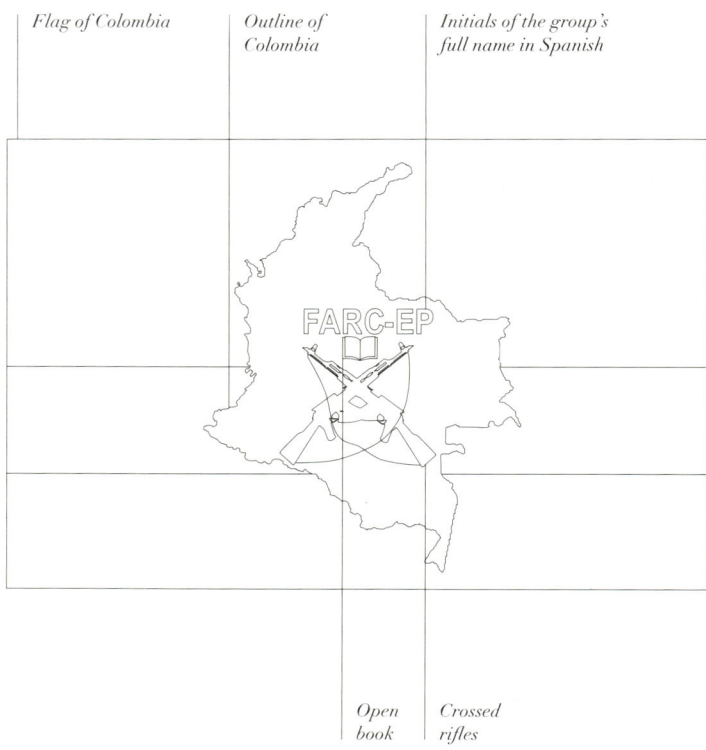

Flag of Colombia

Outline of
Colombia

Initials of the group's
full name in Spanish

Open
book

Crossed
rifles

COLOUR	PANTONE CODE	CMYK	RGB
	012	0.4.100.0	255.231.0
	1797	0.100.99.4	220.8.20
	2756	100.94.0.29	20.27.99
	process black	0.0.0.100	0.0.0

The three colours of the FARC flag – yellow, blue and red – are common to the flags of Colombia and the neighbouring countries of Ecuador and Venezuela, and indicate the region's shared past and identity under Simón Bolívar's Great Colombia (1819–31). The outline of Colombia shows the group's geographical and operational location. The image of a book under the group's initials symbolizes the importance of ideological education. The two crossed assault rifles stand for armed struggle, and, interpreted in combination with the book, convey the message, 'Learn and fight for Colombia'.

57. REVOLUTIONARY ORGANIZATION 17 NOVEMBER (17N)

Name in Greek: Επαναστατική Οργάνωση 17 Νοέμβρη

Transliteration: epanastatiki organosi dekaefta noemvri

Revolutionary Organization 17 November (17N) was formed in Athens, Greece, in 1973 as a leftist organization, with the objective of overthrowing the Greek military dictatorship. The organization's name refers to the date of a bloody suppression by the army of a students' protest against the military junta. The junta collapsed in 1974; but in 1997 17N released a manifesto in which it denounced the post-junta regime as oppressive, authoritarian and complicit in the transformation of Greece into a pawn for foreign interests. The group has opposed imperialism and capitalism, and has promoted a climate of insurrection by targeting symbolic elements of government and business interests, with the stated goal of forcing the American presence out of Greece. It has also been opposed to Turkish presence in Cyprus, and has demanded the withdrawal of Greece from all supranational institutions, including NATO and the European Union.

Although 17N has never had more than twenty-five members, it has been highly efficient, killing twenty-four people between 1975 and 2000. Following a failed bombing in June 2002, nineteen of its members were arrested, fifteen of whom were sentenced to life imprisonment. The group appears to be inactive, but some sources state that its remaining members have been assimilated into »Revolutionary Struggle.

December	**1975**	Assassination of the Athens CIA station chief, Richard Welch
November	**1985**	Remote-controlled bombing next to a Greek police van, killing 1 person and injuring 12 others
May	**1997**	Assassination of the shipping magnate Constantine Peratikos after he threatens to close down his shipyard, which would have left 2000 workers unemployed

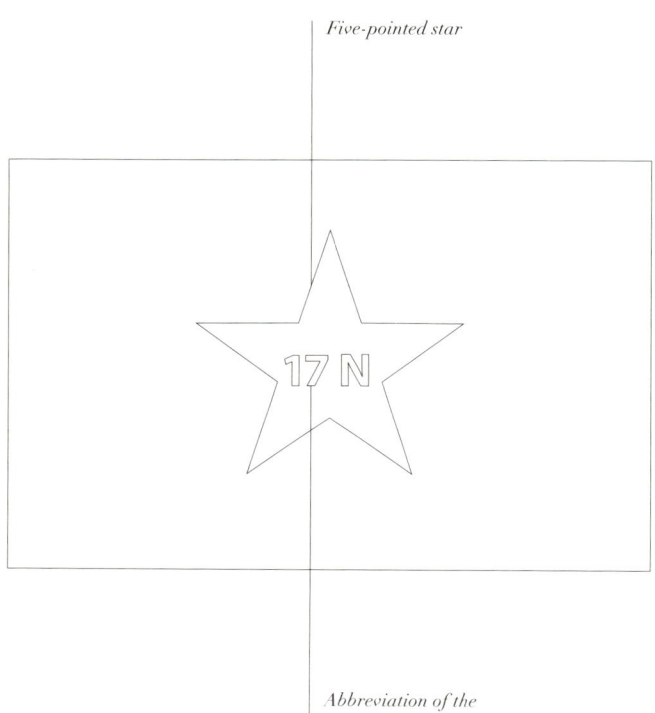

Five-pointed star

*Abbreviation of the
group's name*

COLOUR	PANTONE CODE	CMYK	RGB
	186	0.100.81.4	221.5.43
	116	0.16.100.0	255.211.0

The red flag is a symbol of socialism, communism and general left-wing political orientation, as promoted by 17N. Socialists used the red flag during the political upheavals that swept Europe in 1848 (the 'Year of Revolution'), and it was later associated with communism as a result of its use by the Paris Commune of 1871. The colour evokes a sense of revolution and the blood that has been shed in the struggle for left-wing ideals. The five-pointed yellow star, which is also used in the group's communiqués, represents the unity of workers, peasants, intellectuals, youths and soldiers in building a socialist or communist system.

58. REVOLUTIONARY PEOPLE'S LIBERATION PARTY/FRONT (DHKP/C)

Name in Turkish: Devrinci Halk Kurtulu Partisi/Cephesi

The Revolutionary People's Liberation Party/Front, more widely known by its Turkish-language initials, DHKP/C, is a Marxist-Leninist organization based in Turkey. It was formed in 1978 under the name Devrimci-Sol ('revolutionary left'), and was renamed in 1994. 'Party' refers to the group's political activities, while 'Front' stands for its militant operations.

The DHKP/C is opposed to the current Turkish government, NATO and the United States, including the American presence in Iraq and Afghanistan. Its objectives are to rid Turkey of so-called Western influence through armed struggle and Marxist revolution, and to establish a socialist state. It has fewer than 1000 members, and conducts violent attacks against Turkish government targets and Western interests in Turkey. Modes of attack include assassination, suicide bombing and the use of improvised explosive devices.

August	1991	Assassination of the head of the British Commercial Union in Istanbul, Andrew Blake
January	1996	Assassination of the Turkish businessman Ozdemir Sabanci
July	2004	Suicide bombing of a bus in Istanbul, killing 4 people and wounding 21

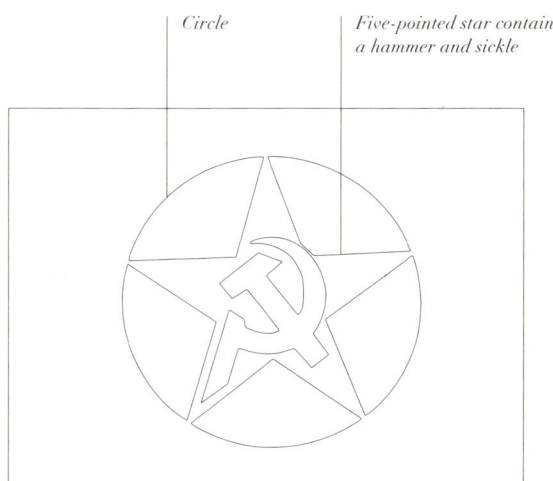

Circle

Five-pointed star containing a hammer and sickle

Hollow five-pointed star

COLOUR	PANTONE CODE	CMYK	RGB
	485	0.97.100.0	177.32.9
	process yellow	0.0.100.0	255.237.0

Logo of the Revolutionary People's Liberation Party

Logo of the Revolutionary People's Liberation Front

The logos used by the DHKP/C are indicative of its Marxist-Leninist ideological foundations. The hammer and sickle are communist symbols used by leftist groups worldwide, as is the five-pointed star. The former represent the worker and the farmer, while the latter represents the unity of the five segments of a socialist society (workers, peasants, intellectuals, soldiers and youth). The red in the logos stands for revolution and the blood that may be shed during the struggle. The yellow is associated with liberalism, a political ideology founded on the ideas of liberty and equality.

59. REVOLUTIONARY STRUGGLE (EA)

Name in Greek: Επαναστατικός Αγώνας
Transliteration: epanastatikos agonas

Revolutionary Struggle (also known by its Greek-language initials, EA) is a Greek radical leftist group inspired by Marxist ideology, insurrectionary anarchism and anarchist communism. The group emerged in Athens in 2003 following the arrests of members of the »Revolutionary Organization 17 November (17N) and the Revolutionary People's Struggle. Analysts believe that the ten remaining members of 17N were assimilated into EA.

In common with 17N, EA is opposed to American foreign policy and to American political and economic influence in Greece. In a statement published in the Greek satirical magazine To Pontiki in 2007, the group expressed discontent with the 'subjugation of the Greek government to US policy' and the presence of Turkish troops in Cyprus; it also condemned the European Union and the parliamentary system of Greece. The group targets symbolic elements of government, security, business and foreign interests in Greece, and has claimed responsibility for bombings, shootings, car bombs, improvised explosive devices and rocket-propelled grenade attacks. In 2010 Greek police arrested six suspected EA members, including the group's leader, Nikos Maziotis.

December	2005	Bomb attack on a finance ministry building in Athens
September	2009	Explosion outside the Athens stock exchange, injuring 1 person and causing significant damage to the area
June	2010	Parcel bomb addressed to the minister of public order explodes in the ministry, killing the minister's aide

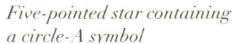

*Five-pointed star containing
a circle-A symbol*

*Five-pointed star featuring the initials
of the group's name in Greek*

COLOUR	PANTONE CODE	CMYK	RGB
	187	0.100.79.20	173.0.33
	process black	0.0.0.100	0.0.0

Logo of EA used on its black-and-white flyers

Logo of EA used for colour and digital publications

The five-pointed star containing the circle-A symbol is used on black-and-white flyers bearing EA's name. The circle-A symbol consists of a capital letter 'A' inside a circle; together they stand for 'Anarchy is Order', an idea propagated by the nineteenth-century French politician and philosopher Pierre-Joseph Proudhon, the first person to call himself an 'anarchist'. The five-pointed star symbolizes the unity of the five social groups (workers, farmers, intellectuals, soldiers and youth) engaged in the struggle for socialism.

The other logo used by the group consists of its Greek-language initials, the capital letters 'E' and 'A', within a red five-pointed star. This logo appears on EA's colour and digital publications.

60.SHINING PATH (SL)

Name in Spanish: Sendero Luminoso

Shining Path (also known by its Spanish-language initials, SL) is a Peruvian leftist revolutionary rebel group that is ideologically based on Maoist principles and connected to the Communist Party of Peru; it was founded by Abimael Guzman, a philosophy professor, in the late 1960s. The group's objective is to overthrow the Peruvian government in order to replace it with a communist peasant revolutionary regime. It furthermore opposes any influence by foreign governments. The group's estimated 300-500 members have conducted bombing campaigns, ambushes, kidnappings and assassinations in an effort to bring down the democratic government, disrupt the economy and ruin the state's reputation among the peasantry and, ultimately, among the whole population.

By 1992, when Guzman was captured and sentenced to life imprisonment, 70,000 people had died in the conflict between SL and government forces. After a period of relative calm, the group has staged a resurgence, fuelled by money from drug trafficking. In 2012 Peru's ministers of defence and the interior both resigned after police efforts to confront the group resulted in several police deaths and allegations of high-level incompetence.

July	1992	Two car bombs in Lima, Peru, killing 18 people and injuring more than 140
October	2008	Bombing in Peru's south-eastern mountains, killing 13 people
April	2012	Kidnapping of 36 workers on gas projects; 23 of them are released in a remote area of the jungle later that day, the rest are freed by Peruvian military forces

Man in camouflage and
balaclava, holding a
stick of dynamite and
an assault rifle

SENDERO LUMINOSO

Name of group in Spanish

Hammer and sickle

COLOUR	PANTONE CODE	CMYK	RGB
■	process black	0.0.0.100	0.0.0

Former logo of SL

Flag of SL

Shining Path uses the classic communist symbol, the hammer and
sickle, on both its logo and its flag. The logo shown here, featuring
an armed man with an assault rifle and a stick of dynamite symbolizing
the group's militancy, has now been replaced by a plainer image of
a hammer and sickle with the group's name around it. The colours of
the flag, red and yellow, are also typical of communism (see p. 109).

61. TALIBAN

Name in Pashto: طالبان

The Taliban is an Islamic extremist group consisting of mujahideen who fought against Soviet troops in Afghanistan in the 1980s, and Afghani Pashtun tribesmen educated in Pakistani religious schools (the group's name means 'students' in Pashto). Its leaders adhere to Wahhabism, an orthodox form of Sunni Islam. The Taliban emerged in 1994 during the Afghan civil war (1992-96); by the end of the war, it controlled the national government. During its rule it harboured the »al-Qaeda founder Osama bin Laden in Afghanistan. By late 2001, when it was ousted by the American military and Afghani opposition forces in response to the al-Qaeda attacks on the United States in September that year, the Taliban had taken control of 95 per cent of the country.

The Taliban's goal was to establish the purest Islamic state in the world. Its rule was characterized by a strict interpretation of sharia law, requiring women to wear head-to-toe burqas while in public, banning television and the internet, and enforcing amputations and public executions for violations of sharia law. Since 2010, the United States has made an effort to agree a negotiated settlement with top Taliban leaders who agree to break ties with al-Qaeda and accept the Afghan constitution.

October	2009	Car bombing in Peshawar, Pakistan, killing 91 people and injuring more than 200 (the Taliban often targets Pakistani authorities in retaliation for their involvement in the war against the group)
August	2011	Shooting down of a NATO helicopter in Wardak province, Afghanistan, killing 38 people
January	2012	Remote-controlled bombing in a market in Jamrud, Pakistan, killing 35 people and injuring 60

*The shahada: 'There is no god but God [Allah],
and Muhammad is His messenger'*

COLOUR	PANTONE CODE	CMYK	RGB
■	process black	0.0.0.100	0.0.0

Before it took power in Afghanistan in 1996, the Taliban used a plain-white flag, featuring no image or writing. In Islam, the white flag (known as <u>al-liwa</u>) is usually a flag of administration. It was the flag of the Umayyad Caliphate (<u>c</u>. 661-750) established after the death of the Prophet Muhammad, and symbolizes the Taliban's aims and identity. In 1996, when it gained control of the Afghan government, the Taliban modified the white flag, adding the shahada, the Muslim declaration of faith. in black writing as a reinforcement of its Islamic identity.

62. ULSTER DEFENCE ASSOCIATION (UDA) / ULSTER FREEDOM FIGHTERS (UFF)

The Ulster Defence Association (UDA) was formed in Northern Ireland in 1971 to unite various loyalist paramilitary groups under one banner, in order to develop a more uniform military training and command structure. The groups that make up the UDA are violently opposed to the unification of Ireland, and want to ensure that Northern Ireland remains a part of the United Kingdom, at times even threatening to fight Britain in order to do so. The UDA also claims to defend the loyalist community of Ulster, the Irish province that contains Northern Ireland, from republican attacks. At its peak in the early 1970s the organization had approximately 40,000 members; its current strength is estimated at 2000-5000.

Of the groups under the UDA banner, the most notable is the Ulster Freedom Fighters (UFF), sometimes referred to as the military wing of the UDA. The UFF was created in the early 1970s to respond to acts of Catholic republican violence against Protestants in Northern Ireland. In 2007 the UDA officially ceased its campaign of violence, ordering the UFF to stand down, but the latter has refused to surrender its weapons.

February	1992	Gun attack on a bookmaker's premises in Belfast, Northern Ireland, killing 5 people and injuring 3
January	2001	Attack on 2 Catholic teenagers in Belfast, using iron bars, a stick and hammers
September	2004	Beating of a man working in a discotheque in Newtownabbey, Northern Ireland, who allegedly tried to prevent UDA members from selling drugs. The man goes into a coma and dies the following year

Red Hand of Ulster

Crown representing
the United Kingdom

Red Hand of Ulster,
fist clenched

Six-pointed star

In Latin:
'Who shall separate us'

Year the group
was founded: 1973

COLOUR	PANTONE CODE	CMYK	RGB
	1797	0.100.99.4	220.8.20
	542	62.22.0.3	97.164.215
	7507	0.10.30.0	97.164.215
	process black	0.0.0.100	0.0.0

Logo of the UDA

Logo of the UFF

The UDA logo features the Red Hand of Ulster, an ancient heraldic symbol used to denote the northern Irish province of Ulster. The crown stands for the group's loyalty to the British crown. The motto at the bottom of the logo, translated from the Latin as 'Who shall separate us', refers to the knightly Order of St Patrick, established in 1783 by George III as the Irish equivalent of the Order of the Garter, the most senior British order of chivalry. The motto is derived from the biblical verse Romans 8:35, and signifies the historic ties that bind Northern Ireland to the United Kingdom.

The UFF logo features a clenched-fist version of the Red Hand of Ulster, conveying courage, strength and militancy, and symbolizing the UFF's commitment to the use of violence. The fist sits within a six-pointed star representing the six counties of Northern Ireland. The wreath surrounding the logo stands for victory (of the eternal spirit) over death. In the star's bottom point, the number 73 refers to 1973, the year the group was formed.

63. UNITED LIBERATION FRONT OF ASSAM (ULFA)

The United Liberation Front of Assam (ULFA) was founded in 1979 with the aim of establishing Assam, a state in north-eastern India, as a sovereign socialist nation. The group claims to represent all people struggling for an independent Assam, irrespective of race, tribe, caste or religion.

The ULFA is estimated to have some 3000 members, and has training camps in Bangladesh and southern Bhutan. After initially being dormant, it began raising funds in 1986, extorting money from traders, businesspeople, and Indian and foreign-owned tea gardens. From 1990 the group increased its militant activities. It has assassinated political opponents, attacked law-enforcement and security forces, and attempted to destroy rail tracks and other infrastructure. Researchers in the field of terrorism studies state that the ULFA cooperates strategically with the »National Democratic Front of Bodoland.

July	1991	Kidnapping for ransom of 14 people in Assam over the course of the month
March	2003	Explosion at a petrol reservoir at the Digboi oil refinery, Assam, causing immense property loss
March	2003	Roadside bomb explosion under a passenger bus in the Goalpara district of Assam, killing 6 people and injuring 55

Rising sun

UNITED LIBERATION FRONT OF ASOM

COLOUR	PANTONE CODE	CMYK	RGB
	1797	0.100.99.4	220.8.20
	process black	0.0.0.100	0.0.0

UNITED LIBERATION FRONT OF ASOM

Logo of the ULFA

Flag of the ULFA

The symbol of the ULFA is a rising red sun, which stands for a new beginning, referring to an independent Assam. The state officially changed the spelling of its name to Asom, as used here, in 2006.

64. UNITED NATIONAL LIBERATION FRONT (UNLF)

The United National Liberation Front (UNLF) was founded in 1964 with the aim of establishing an independent Manipur nation (the region is a state in north-eastern India) with a socialist government. It was established as a non-violent group, but in 1990 openly stated that it would take up arms in order to achieve its goals. The group formed an armed wing, the Manipur People's Army.

With an estimated cadre strength of 1500-3500, most of whom are ethnic Meiteis (the majority ethnic group of Manipur), the UNLF is the most potent militant group in the state. Many of its members are trained in the use of sophisticated weapons, and the group has been reported as having training camps in Myanmar and Bangladesh.

The UNLF targets Indian army and security personnel, and enforces a campaign of social reform in Manipur. It takes vigilante action against alcoholism, gambling and drug abuse, and has also claimed to have executed scores of rapists.

February	1999	Killing of nine Indian security-force personnel in the Churachandpur district of Manipur
March	2008	Grenade attack on military personnel in Imphal, the capital of Manipur, injuring 9 soldiers
December	2010	Ambush of a military division in the Chandel district of Manipur, injuring 6 soldiers

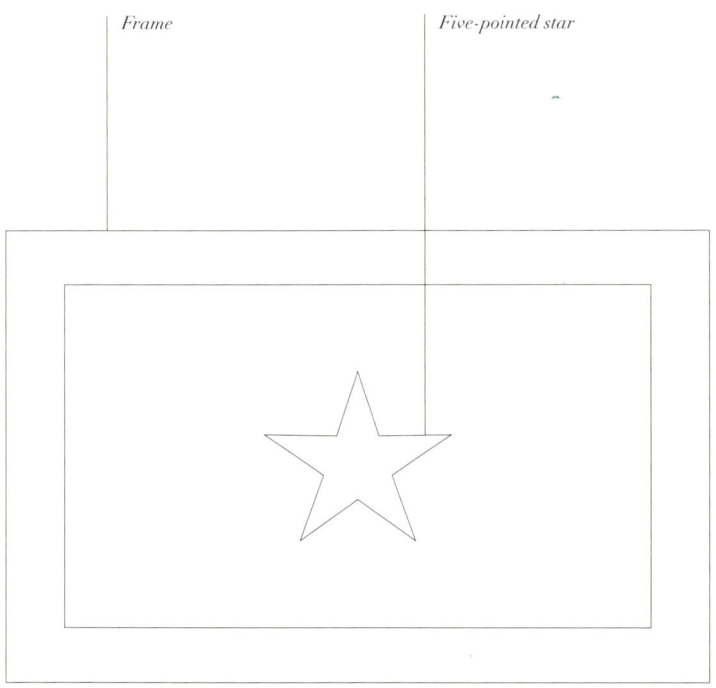

Frame *Five-pointed star*

COLOUR	PANTONE CODE	CMYK	RGB
	032	0.90.86.0	29.29.27

Red is the traditional colour of socialism. In the UNLF flag, the red five-pointed star symbolizes the unity of the Manipur people in the fight for an independent state based on socialist principles. The socialist principles of the group are further reinforced by the use of a red frame.

65. UNITED SELF-DEFENCE FORCES OF COLOMBIA (AUC)

Name in Spanish: Autodefensas Unidas de Colombia

The United Self-Defence Forces of Colombia (better known by its Spanish-language initials, AUC) was founded in 1997 as an umbrella organization of independent far-right paramilitary groups in Colombia. Its objective is to protect the economic interests of Colombian economic elites and local communities threatened by communist-inspired insurgent groups, primarily the »Revolutionary Armed Forces of Colombia (FARC) and the »National Liberation Army (ELN). The AUC engages guerrilla combat units and assassinates suspected supporters of insurgents. Several groups within the AUC raise funds through extortion and by protecting cocaine laboratory operations.

In the early 1990s the AUC cooperated with the Colombian military, but owing to the group's financial connections to drug cartels, the military officially ended the cooperation. In 2004 the Colombian government began peace talks with the AUC on the disarmament of the organization's cells and their integration into the Colombian army. According to the Colombian government, by 2006 more than 27,000 paramilitaries had submitted their weapons. However, several units refused to disarm and continued their activities. The last remaining leaders of an AUC unit were captured in 2012 by Venezuelan authorities.

August	2007	Attack on the village of Santa Tomas, Colombia, killing 12 people for alleged cooperation with leftist rebels
September	2005	Raid in a rural area in the Falan Municipality, Colombia, killing 11 people and injuring 2
October	2001	Members of the Black Eagles unit kill 3 people and injure 1 in Riosucio, Colombia

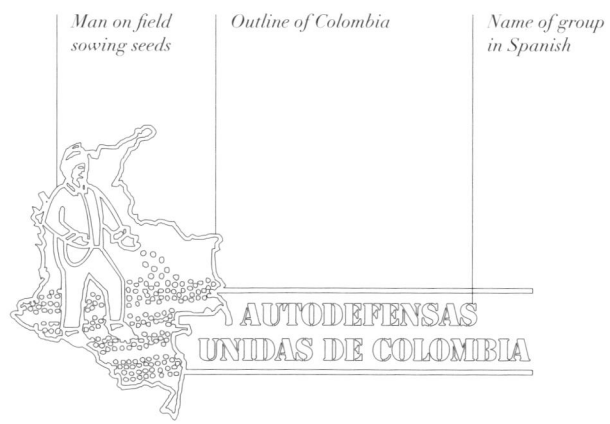

Man on field
sowing seeds

Outline of Colombia

Name of group
in Spanish

AUTODEFENSAS
UNIDAS DE COLOMBIA

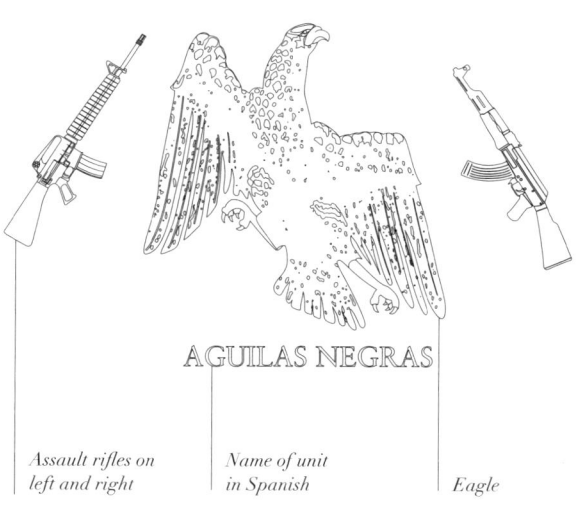

AGUILAS NEGRAS

Assault rifles on
left and right

Name of unit
in Spanish

Eagle

COLOUR	PANTONE CODE	CMYK	RGB
	2726	79.66.0.0	78.92.166
	process black	0.0.0.100	0.0.0

Logo of the AUC

AGUILAS NEGRAS

Logo of the AUC's Black Eagles unit

The AUC logo features an outline of Colombia, showing the geographical location and operational focus of the group. The image of a man seeding a field is a metaphor for reclaiming land occupied by left-wing radical groups. The logo of the AUC's Black Eagles unit features an eagle, a widely used symbol in heraldry. As a bird of prey, the eagle is regarded as the king of the air. The Black Eagles was one of the AUC units that refused to disarm; in this sense, the eagle symbolizes courage and vision. The continuation of armed struggle is further reinforced by illustrations of assault rifles.

MAIN EVENTS TIMELINE

This timeline covers a selection of the most lethal and significant terrorist attacks executed since 1970, both by groups featured in this book (indicated by the symbol » in front of the group's name) and by groups not featured in this book. A page reference indicates that details of the attack have been given on that page.

6 October
The Egyptian president, Anwar al-Sadat, is assassinated during a military parade with the participation of the »Muslim Brotherhood and »Islamic Jihad Movement in Palestine

21 November
The Irish republican revolutionary group Irish Republican Army (IRA) plants bombs in 2 pubs in Birmingham, killing 21 people and injuring some 200

6 September
Four airliners are hijacked by members of the »Popular Front for the Liberation of Palestine (see p. 261)

1970	1973	1974	1975	1981	1983

20 December
The Spanish prime minister is assassinated by members of »Basque Fatherland and Liberty (see p. 89)

23 December
The Athens CIA station chief is assassinated by members of the »Revolutionary Organization 17 November (see p. 283)

23 October
American and French military bases in Lebanon are attacked by a suicide bomber for »Hezbollah (see p. 145)

27 June

An Air India flight is destroyed by a bomb planted by members of »Babbar Khalsa (see p. 85)

7 October

A cruise ship is hijacked and 1 of its passengers murdered by members of the »Palestine Liberation Front (see p. 253)

21 December

Pan American World Airlines Flight 103 from London to New York is destroyed in flight by a bomb and crashes into the village of Lockerbie in Scotland, killing all 259 people on board and 11 people on the ground. In 2003 Libya accepted responsibility for the attack and paid reparation to the victims

17 March

A suicide bomber for »Hezbollah attacks the Israeli embassy in Buenos Aires, Argentina, killing 29 people and injuring 242

| 1985 | 1986 | 1988 | 1991 | 1992 | 1993 |

---

6 September

Members of the Palestinian militant group Abu Nidal Organization attack a synagogue in Istanbul, killing 21 people before killing themselves

21 May

A suicide bomber for the »Liberation Tigers of Tamil Eelam assassinates the former Indian prime minister Rajiv Gandhi in southern India; some 15 others are killed

26 February

A car bomb is detonated at the World Trade Center, New York, in retaliation for American aid to Israel, killing 6 people and injuring more than 1000. Among the 7 men convicted of the attack is Omar Abdel-Rahman, the spiritual leader of »Gama'a al-Islamiyya

23 February
»Al-Qaeda issues
a fatwa urging the
murder of Americans

7 March
Members of
the Islamic
fundamentalist group
Harakat ul-Jihad-
i-Islami detonate
two bombs at a
political meeting in
Bangladesh, killing
10 people and
injuring 75

9 February
The IRA breaks a
17-month ceasefire
and detonates a
bomb in Docklands,
London, killing
2 people and
injuring more
than 100

20 March
Sarin nerve gas
is released in the
Tokyo subway system
by members of »Aum
Shinrikyo (see p. 81)

4 November
The Israeli
prime minister is
assassinated by a
member of »Kahane
Chai (see p. 193)

25 February
Public buses in
Jerusalem are
bombed by »Hamas
(see p. 129)

7 August
American embassies
in Kenya and
Tanzania are bombed
by members of »al-
Qaeda (see p. 49)

1994   1995   1996   1997   1998

25 February
An American-born
supporter of Kach
(»Kahane Chai/Kach)
opens fire in a West
Bank mosque (p. 193)

31 January
Members of the
»Liberation Tigers
of Tamil Eelam
attack the Central
Bank in Colombo, Sri
Lanka, with firearms
and a suicide truck
bomb, killing 90
people and injuring
more than 1400

17 November
More than 60
tourists and local
people are killed
in Luxor, Egypt, by
members of »Gama'a
al-Islamiyya
(see p. 115)

24 July
A shopping centre in Jerusalem is attacked by a suicide bomber for »Hamas, causing 12 deaths and injuries to more than 120 people

11 September
Four American domestic flights are hijacked and crashed by members of »al-Qaeda; the World Trade Center, New York, is destroyed (see p. 49)

3 August
A car bomb is detonated in Ealing Broadway, west London, by members of the »Real Irish Republican Army, injuring 6 people

12 October
»Al-Qaeda suicide bombers attack the US Navy destroyer USS Cole in Yemen, killing 17 sailors

1999   2000   2001

20 May
In Italy, members of the »Brigate Rosse per la Costruzione del Partito Comunista Combattente assassinate Massimo D'Antona, a senior adviser to the prime minister

1 June
A nightclub in Tel Aviv, Israel, is destroyed by a suicide bomber for the »Izz ad-Din al-Qassam Brigades (see p. 181)

16 August
More than 10 people are killed in the village of Santo Tomas, Colombia, by members of the »United Self-Defence Forces of Colombia for alleged cooperation with leftist rebels

5 March

An underground car
park in Cucuta,
Colombia, is bombed
by the »National
Liberation Army
(see p. 241)

12 October

Two car bombs are
detonated in Kuta,
Bali, by members of
the South-East Asian
militant Islamist
organization Jemaah
Islamiyah, killing
202 people and
injuring more
than 209

15 March

A police building in
Indian-administered
Kashmir is attacked
by militants for
»Harakat ul-Mujahideen,
»Hizbul Mujahideen
and the related
Harakat
ul-Jihad-i-Islami
(see p. 141)

2002   2003

23 February

Colombian
presidential
candidate Ingrid
Betancourt is
kidnapped by the
»Revolutionary Armed
Forces of Colombia
(see p. 279)

23 October

Some 50 Islamist
militants fighting
for an independent
Chechnya seize a
theatre in Moscow,
taking more than
800 people hostage.
After a 2^{1}/$_{2}$-day
siege, all the
militants and more
than 120 hostages
are killed by
Russian forces

20 November

In Istanbul,
Turkey, suicide
bombers attack the
headquarters of
HSBC bank and the
British consulate;
both the »Great
Eastern Islamic
Raiders Front
and »al-Qaeda
are suspected by
analysts of being
responsible (see
p. 119)

1 September

Separatist Chechen militants occupy a school in Beslan, Russia, taking more than 1000 hostages. More than 330 people are killed, and 770 injured, as Russian forces retake the school

2 November

The Dutch film-maker Theo van Gogh is assassinated in Amsterdam by a member of the »Hofstadgroep (see p. 159)

28 February

In India, a truck crowded with anti-Maoist villagers is bombed by members of the »Communist Party of India (Maoist) (see p. 101)

11 July

In Mumbai, India, commuter trains are bombed by members of »Lashkar-e-Tayyiba (see p. 209)

12 July

An Israeli army patrol is attacked by members of »Hezbollah (see p. 145)

6 September

In Algeria, a suicide bomber for »al-Qaeda in the Islamic Maghreb attempts to assassinate the Algerian president (see p. 63)

27 December

Former Pakistani prime minister Benazir Bhutto and 20 others are killed at an election rally in Rawalpindi, Pakistan, by a suicide attacker for »Lashkar-e-Tayyiba

---

2004	2005	2006	2007

---

1 February

The offices of the Kurdistan Democratic Party and the Patriotic Union of Kurdistan in Irbil, Iraq, are attacked by »Ansar al-Islam (see p. 69)

22 May

The »Revolutionary Armed Forces of Colombia detonate a bomb in a discotheque in Apartado, Colombia, killing 6 people and injuring 82

4 May

In Irbil, Iraq, a suicide bomber for »Ansar al-Islam kills 69 people and injures 110

7 July

In London, suicide bombers for »al-Qaeda detonate their bombs on the transport system (see p. 49)

14 February

In Zahedan, Iran, members of »Jundallah detonate a car bomb near a bus carrying troops of Iran's Army of the Guardians of the Islamic Revolution (Revolutionary Guards), killing 11 people and injuring 34

17 February
In Kandahar, Afghanistan, a suicide bomber for the »Taliban kills some 80 people

13 May
Bombs are detonated in Jaipur, India, by members of »Indian Mujahideen (see p. 167)

26 November
In Mumbai, India, »Lashkar-e-Tayyiba undertakes coordinated deadly attacks (see p. 209)

29 July
»Basque Fatherland and Liberty detonate a car bomb in Burgos, Spain (p. 89)

18 October
Suicide bomb attack in Pishin, Iran, for »Jundallah (see p. 189)

11 July
In Kampala, Uganda, two suicide bombers for »Harakat al-Shabaab al-Mujahideen kill 74 people and injure more than 70

24 August
A hotel in Mogadishu, Somalia, is attacked by two suicide bombers for »Harakat al-Shabaab al-Mujahideen (see p. 135)

2008   2009   2010

4 February
Near Barbacoas, Colombia, 17 people are stabbed to death by members of the »Revolutionary Armed Forces of Colombia

29 March
Two Moscow subway stations are attacked by suicide bombers for the »Caucasus Emirate (see p. 97)

16 April
In Quetta, Pakistan, a suicide bomber for the Sunni militant organization Lashkar-e-Jhangvi opens fire in a hospital and then detonates his bomb, killing 12 people and injuring 40

14 December
A mosque in Chabahar, Iran, is attacked by suicide bombers for »Jundallah (see p. 189)

18 January

In Tikrit, Iraq, a
suicide bomber for
»al-Qaeda in Iraq
kills 50 people and
injures 150

24 January

Moscow's Domodedovo
International
Airport is attacked
by a suicide bomber
for the »Caucasus
Emirate (p. 97)

4 October

A government
building in
Mogadishu, Somalia,
is attacked by a
suicide car-bomber for
»Harakat al-Shabaab
al-Mujahideen; 139
people are killed and
93 injured

2011   **2012**

---

3 April

A Sufi shrine
in Dera Ghazi
Khan, Pakistan,
is attacked by
a suicide bomber
for the Islamist
militant network
Tehrik-e Taliban
Pakistan; 50 people
are killed and more
than 100 injured

20 March

Coordinated bomb
attacks are launched
in 19 towns and
cities in Iraq by
the Sunni umbrella
organization the
Islamic State of
Iraq (see pp. 53
and 61), killing
some 50 people
and injuring more
than 250

GLOSSARY

The symbol » indicates a term defined in the glossary.

anarchist communism

A political theory that advocates the abolition of the state, of money and of private property, and favours common ownership of the means of production, direct democracy and a lack of hierarchy.

caliphate

A theocratic pan-Islamic government under which both religious and political affairs are governed by »sharia law. Historic caliphates have included the Umayyad Caliphate (c. 661-750) established after the death of the Prophet Muhammad in 632; the Abbasid Caliphate (750-1258), which had its capital in Baghdad (in modern Iraq); and the Ottoman Caliphate established by Turkish tribes in the thirteenth century.

communism

A theory or system of social organization, derived from »Marxism, in which all property is owned by the community and each person contributes and receives according to ability and needs.

Deobandi

A radical movement in »Islam that rejects all Western influence and seeks to return to classical Islam.

ethno-nationalism

A strain of »nationalism that is defined by the desire of an ethnic community to have absolute authority over its own political, economic and social affairs.

fatwa

A juristic ruling on a point of Islamic law. In »Sunni Islam it is not binding, whereas in »Shia Islam it can be.

the Five Pillars of Islam

Five basic acts in »Islam, considered to be mandatory by believers: the »shahada; daily prayers; the giving of alms; fasting during Ramadan (the ninth month of the Islamic calendar); and the pilgrimage to Mecca at least once in a lifetime.

Hinduism

The predominant religion of the Indian subcontinent. It is formed of diverse traditions, includes the worship of a large pantheon of deities, and has no single founder; it has its roots in the twelfth century BC.

insurrectionary anarchism

A left-wing revolutionary theory that advocates a refusal to negotiate or compromise with class enemies, and puts value in acts of violence.

Islam

The religion of Muslims. Islam is a monotheistic faith regarded as having been revealed in the early seventh century through Muhammad (c. 570 – c. 632), the prophet of Allah (God). The term is also used to signify the Muslim world.

jihad/jihadist

Jihad is the Arabic word for 'struggle'. It has a variety of interpretations, including spiritual struggle for moral purity; trying to correct wrong and support right by voice and deeds; and military war against non-Muslims with the aim of spreading Islam. A jihadist is a Muslim who is involved in jihad as military war.

Leninism

»Marxism as interpreted by Vladimir Ilyich Lenin, the premier of the Soviet Union from 1922 to 1924, in relation to the social and political conditions of the agrarian Russian empire of the early twentieth century

liberation theology

A political movement in Christian theology that interprets the teachings of Jesus Christ in terms of a liberation from unjust economic, political or social conditions.

loyalist

The term used to describe a supporter of Northern Ireland's status as part of the United Kingdom.

Maoism

A political theory derived from the »communist doctrines of Mao Zedong, the Chinese head of state from 1949 to 1959.

Marxism

The political and economic theories of Karl Marx (1818-1883) and Friedrich Engels (1820-1895), later developed to form the basis for the theory and practice of »communism.

mujahideen

An »Islamic guerrilla fighter.

nationalism/nationalist

Nationalism refers to the advocacy of political independence for a particular country or ethnic group. In an Irish context, a nationalist is a supporter of the unification of Northern Ireland (which is part of the United Kingdom) and the Republic of Ireland.

open sources

The term refers to sources of information that are freely accessible, such as newspapers, books, internet blogs, and radio and television reports.

Qur'an

The sacred book of »Islam, believed by Muslims to be the word of God as dictated to the Prophet Muhammad in the early seventh century, and written down in Arabic.

republican

In an Irish context, a republican advocates a united Republic of Ireland that would include Northern Ireland (which is part of the United Kingdom); in this context, republicans are also known as »nationalists.

Salafiyya (also known as Salafism)

A radical movement in »Islam that advocates a return to the pure roots of Islam, and the restoration of the traditional beliefs and practices that prevailed during the time of the Prophet Muhammad (the seventh century).

shahada

The Muslim declaration of faith in the oneness of God and acceptance of Muhammad as God's prophet: 'There is no god but God [Allah], and Muhammad is His messenger.' The word comes from the Arabic for the verb 'to witness'.

sharia

The traditional canon of the moral codes and religious laws of »Islam, based on the teachings of the »Qur'an and the traditions of the Prophet Muhammad.

Shia

A denomination of »Islam that broke away from »Sunni Islam, the main denomination, in 657.

Sikhism

A monotheistic religion founded in the Punjab region of eastern Pakistan and northern India in the fifteenth century by Guru Nanak Nev. Most of its followers live in India, where they make up just under 2 per cent of the population.

socialism

A political and economic theory of social organization in which the means of production, distribution and exchange are owned or regulated by the community as a whole.

Sunni

The largest branch of »Islam, representing 80-90 per cent of Muslims today.

takbir

The Arabic term for the Arabic phrase Allahu Akbar ('God is [the] Greatest'), used by Muslims as an expression of faith; in prayer; in times of distress; and to express celebration or victory, determination or defiance.

unionist

The term used to describe a supporter of the continuation of the political union of Northern Ireland with the United Kingdom.

Wahhabism

A conservative and puritanical form of »Sunni Islam, instigated in the eighteenth century by the theologian Muhammad ibn Abd al-Wahhab. It is predominant in Saudi Arabia.

SOURCES

Lists of designated terrorist organizations

Australia:
ema.gov.au/agd/www/nationalsecurity.nsf/
AllDocs/95FB057CA3DECF30CA256FAB001F7FBD?
OpenDocument
(accessed 18 October 2012)

European Union:
eur-lex.europa.eu/LexUriServ/LexUriServ.do?
uri=OJ:L:2009:023:0037:0042:EN:PDF
(accessed 18 October 2012)

India:
mha.gov.in/uniquepage.asp?Id_Pk=292
(accessed 18 October 2012)

Russia:
nak.fsb.ru/nac/ter_org.htm
(accessed 18 October 2012)

United States:
state.gov/j/ct/rls/other/des/123085.htm
(accessed 18 October 2012)

Books

Sean K. Anderson and Stephen Sloan,
Historical Dictionary of Terrorism, Plymouth
(Scarecrow Press) 2009

Muhammad Muhsin Khan, The Noble Qur'an:
Transliteration in Roman Script and English
Translation of the Meanings, Riyadh
(Darussalam Publishers and Distributors) 2002

Police National Legal Database, Blackstone's
Counter-terrorism Handbook, Oxford (Oxford
University Press) 2010

Michael R. Ronczkowski, Terrorism and
Organized Hate Crime: Intelligence Gathering,
Analysis and Investigations, London (CRC
Press) 2006

Documents Online

'Chapter 6. Foreign Terrorism Organizations'
(US Department of State, Bureau of
Counterterrorism, 2010), state.gov/j/ct/rls/
crt/2010/170264.htm
(accessed 14 September 2012)

'The Islamic Imagery Project:
Visual Motifs in Jihadi Internet Propaganda'
(Combating Terrorism Center, Department
of Social Sciences, United States Military
Academy, 2006), ctc.usma.edu/posts/the-
islamic-imagery-project
(accessed 14 September 2012)

Databases

Anti-Defamation League: adl.org

Australian National Security:
nationalsecurity.gov.au

Council on Foreign Relations: cfr.org

Global Security: globalsecurity.org

IHS Jane's: janes.com

International Centre for Political Violence
and Terrorism Research: pvtr.org

International Crisis Group: crisisgroup.org

The Jamestown Foundation: jamestown.org

Meir Amit Intelligence and Terrorism
Information Center: terrorism-info.org.il

South Asia Terrorism Portal: satp.org

START – The National Consortium for
the Study of Terrorism and Responses
to Terrorism: start.umd.edu/start

Strategic Studies Institute,
United States Army War College:
strategicstudiesinstitute.army.mil

INDEX

First published 2013 by
Merrell Publishers, London
and New York

Merrell Publishers Limited
81 Southwark Street
London SE1 0HX

merrellpublishers.com

Text and design copyright © 2013
Artur Beifuss and
Francesco Trivini Bellini
Illustrations copyright © 2013 the
respective organizations
Finished layout and files copyright
© 2013 Merrell Publishers Limited

All rights reserved. No part of
this publication may be reproduced,
stored in a retrieval system or
transmitted, in any form or by
any means, electronic, mechanical,
photocopying, recording or otherwise,
without the prior written permission
of the publisher.

British Library Cataloguing-in-
Publication Data. A catalogue record
for this book is available from the
British Library.

ISBN 978-1-8589-4601-6

Artur Beifuss is a journalist and
formerly worked for the United Nations
as a counter-terrorism analyst.

Francesco Trivini Bellini is a creative
director who has developed the branding
identity of various companies and
cultural institutions.

Steven Heller is a former Art Director
at the New York Times, and the author
or co-author of more than 120 books on
design and popular culture.

Authors' acknowledgements
We wish to express our gratitude to
the people who inspired us to write
this book and made it possible. In
particular, we thank: Madison Li and
Annemarie Van Kersen; Anna Corraini;
Gianfranco Maria Trivini Bellini;
Carla Balboni and Simona Gottshalk;
Robert, Galina and Lilia Beifuss;
Emilia Hein; Meriam Daadouche, Graham
Cushway and Lari Nyroos.

Produced by Merrell Publishers Limited
Project manager: Marion Moisy
Art editor: Alexandre Coco
Art asssistants: Tom Lobo Brennan,
James Drayson and Elena Mosca
Indexer: Hilary Bird

Printed and bound in China